Remembrances Under the Shadow of the Mango Tree

A true story of survival, empowerment and resilience while experiencing the worst forms of abuse

By Ramonita Rodriguez

Remembrances under the Shadow of the Mango Tree
Copyright © 2013 by Ramonita Rodriguez

ISBN:9781494907303

U.S. Retail Price: $9:08

Printed in USA by CreateSpace

Dedication

This book is dedicated to my family, my children, and my loving spouse, Otilio, the love of my life, whose help, positive words and unending love and acceptance has always been my main motivator. This book is also dedicated to my sisters Tina, Betty, Lydia, and Maria...the pillars of strength in the family and my heroines...to my mom...the glue that kept it all together even in the most terrible times. To Angel and Candy...my special gifts from God and my inspiration in my earnest desire to leave them a legacy...this story is for you. To my beloved husband Otilio, the love of my life...to my strong brothers Junior, Oscar (RIP), Jose Bibiano, Edwin and Joseph Q. And last but not least, my Lord and Savior...the one who made this book possible, the one who allowed me to walk in the darkness of the valley of death and back while holding me lovingly in His arms...Without you...it could not have been done...with you, all is possible.

Philippians 4:13 NIV
I can do all this through him who gives me strength.

Table of Contents

Preface

I always knew that I had to write my herstory…always heard about others writing their story, anecdotes of a time long past gone, memories of good and evil, laughter and tears, hope and despair, strength and weakness…and I knew that I had a herstory, that my herstory was unique because it was mine and mine only and that the events described here, really happened. They are not a figment of my imagination…it has been a lifetime of remembrances, but now…it is here, for the world to know and for my heart to finally rest. This is my story, in my own words. Some of the names have been changed to protect the innocent and the guilty ones. I have learned to forgive, and while learning to forgive, I finally learned how to set free the ghosts of a lifetime of abuse and despair…so now I can finally say that I learned to live.

Introduction

If you are or at one time in your life were the victim of abuse or were ever victimized emotionally, sexually, or physically by those unknown to you or those you trusted, then this book is for you. It is my deepest desire that you also tell your story and allow the wounds to heal, learn the power within you, the power or the gift of forgiveness, and let yourself be free. Let yourself find your inner strength and find purpose in your life, for you were born with a purpose.

Chapter 1

Farewell Sweet Georgia...and Welcome to North Carolina

February 2011...after many years, months, weeks of unknown expectations, trails of tears, ambivalent emotions, and so many thoughts and feelings, moving day is finally here. After living in Georgia for over twenty years, life as I have known it for these past twenty-one years will take an unfamiliar turn.

Ring! Riiiiiiing! The phone startled me from my comfy bed as the movers called to inform that they were on their merry way and to ask for precise directions. They would make it there if they were lucky, I must repeat lucky because in the ten years at our house, everyone coming to the house for whatever reason, guests, family, service men, they all had lost their way to the house, lost their way through the long, hazy, winding country roads that seemed to go on forever until they reached the fork in the road and, of course, took the wrong turn and ended up by the dilapidated bridge leading to another county. Of course, they never declined the amicable request to go meet them by the main highway to bring them to the house.

Soon, they were to be at the house and lo and behold, to my frazzled surprise, two sets of teams of reliable moving technicians each consisting of maybe four or five, strong, muscular moving specialists were readily knocking at the front door, eager and ready to earn their daily hard-earned cash and equipped to start the monotonous job of opening cardboard boxes; laying soiled, heavy, malodorous grey and blue packing mats all over the rooms; and whacking the metal, heavy duty cardboard cutters as they attempted to open the innumerable boxes of sticky packing tape. This filled our kitchen with familiar sounds, and their journey was about to begin...

It had been two long months since being in NC, and in my mind, it has seemed like an eternity. There were hundreds of boxes to unpack, rooms to decorate, stuff to move, and I was physically and emotionally numb and tired. I walked around my new home, arms to my side. I was lost in my thoughts, and I knew that I was so tired. I had no energy left...the ugly monster trapped inside my mind appeared to be lurking in every cell of blood, every nook and cranny of my flesh, in every ligament. At times, this monster was so overpowering and menacing that it seemed that it was vacuuming every gleam of energy left on my seemingly lethargic, lifeless body. I talked out loud, trying to reason with the lurking monster to leave, to leave me alone, to go on, to disappear, and to be swallowed to never come out again, but its dwindling claws just inflicted deeper pain, and her clamor kept falling on deaf ears...I pleaded, asking it to leave her alone, but my pleas were not heard.

This monster had a mind of its own and wanted to keep me down, to crush me and suck every drop of my blood, every last breath, but I kept fighting, kept battling, and I am not one to give up easily.

I got up slowly, and every day, the battle raged on. I struggled, I earnestly tried to cajole it, I screamed at it, even arguing with it. My daily struggles continued, and I saw a light at the end of the tunnel, which makes me very happy. I had to remind myself over and over again that this struggle must continue, my fight must go on, and that my final desire is to bury the monster. I laughed inside, a burst of sunshine in my painful life, and this was because the thought of burying my tormentor makes me so happy, so every day, I got up to try to smile. I was and am thankful for the pain and the struggles inside...I smiled at myself in the mirror, although smiling made my body cringe with pain, and my body is in constant pain, the final outcome was the longing cry and the slow receding of the monster, trying to shake down my innermost foundation.

I have given this monster a name, DISEASE, and it does not goes away easily, but it is not taking over me, and I know that I must repeat this over and over to remind myself of better days ahead.

I have to honestly admit that I had tried every method within my power, and finally I started making arrangements to see different doctors, specialists with the knowledge, skills, and tools to make the monster at least hide away for a while. It is not going away, but I can make it weaker and not let it take over my life and my body. The challenges and struggles in the future will certainly make this monster super happy, but I cannot let it take complete control.

In NC everything is so different, even referrals to other specialists take time. Finally I go see my primary care doctor. The sadness, tears, and desperation that are the special traits of the monster within me try to take over, and at last the doctor saw what I had been trying to tell him. It had been so many years of pent up frustrations, emotions, pains, hurts, and weakness until finally I realized that I needed help. I could not and cannot battle this war alone, too many years of not telling anyone, keeping the pain inside, suffering alone. This was the time to share that pain with someone.

Ms. Rose has a way with words…she was such a godsend. She is such an easygoing kind of person, and her life is in some ways similar to mine. She has seen the strength, resiliency, and will to live within me and has slowly been helping me on the road to recovery. Her choices of words pack such power, and she is not judging me, but trying to help me become a stronger, better

person…

Chapter 2

October 1953

As I felt the rush of pure, fresh air gushing into my lungs, I knew that my birthday had arrived. It was a cool crisp early morning in October 1953...I always said 1953 because that is what Mom told me...but oftentimes she would err and said that I was born in 1952. She was living in an old, dilapidated shack in the community of Los Indios, Guayanilla. Times for Mom had been hard and harder still with the arrival of a newborn baby girl whom she detested; those were her words that I often heard and they are still somewhere in the back of my mind. Yes, I grew up hearing the recounts over and over of how she wished that I had never been born, how it would have been much easier for her if I had stayed somewhere in the celestial orbs hanging around heavenly bodies instead of deciding to make such an unwelcome entrance into my earthly home. Her stinging words still buzz, and their echoes still ring in my ears like the annoying flyby of the mosquitoes at dusk...but now they are just words...probably words spoken out of anger, ignorance, sheer desperation, and helplessness.

Yes, I was an unwanted, unplanned pregnancy and an unwanted child as well, but I made the most of it. My birth was predetermined by the mercy of a loving God, because my mother had other plans for me altogether or so I always thought. I preferred to give her the benefit of the doubt, and I knew that the task of raising me seemed insurmountable.

As far back as I could remember, my mother told me the herstory of my birth. She always said that she never loved my father and after her first three boys were yanked from her bosom, she vowed not to ever profess even a hint of affection toward my biological father. He was aware of this...he was a hopeless drunkard, a gambler, way too old for her, almost twenty-three years her senior; his first love had always been alcohol. Her story continued and went back nine months earlier when she told me that she was at home readying to go to bed when she heard a loud knock at the door. Upon getting a robe and opening the door, she came face to face with a boisterous, drunken man, the man whom she had ran off with years before to get married but they never did. That man was my father, who came in in the middle of the night, in a jealous and drunken rage grabbed my mother by the neck and started yelling obscenities at her while closing the main door behind him. Mom said that he was not only drunk, but angry at her constant rejections of him, and he wanted sex. He was not going to take no for an answer, and he was not going away. The story continues regarding how he managed to pull out a small gun out hidden in his belt and proceeded to rape her…while my older siblings slept. She was terrified not only for her life, but for the little ones sleeping in cots in the other room. She acquiesced and submitted to his violent advances, out of sheer terror, to save her own skin, and to save her children from violence and harm.

I really think that from the moment I opened my own little eyes and my ears, this violent recount was drilled into me, the hatred and vengeance stemming from this episode expanding like the ocean as it was retold over and over. At times I wanted to cover my ears so as not to listen to my mother's accounts of my conception, but she made sure and made it her business that I knew that I was not a wanted or loved child. I made it my business to prove her wrong all along. I think that while growing up and as a small child, my purpose was to prove to my mother that she had been wrong about me...that I belonged in this world and I would make my earnest efforts to prove her wrong.

She told me how bad and sick she felt the night I was born. She had sent my two oldest siblings Ed and Tina to stay with their respective biological father, Don Pedro. The only souls in the little shack were her and my older sister Betty, who had been born sickly and was asleep on a nearby cot. She knew that the birthing process was getting close, so she sent out word to her neighbor to send for the local midwife. But the midwife never arrived and the only person present upon my birth was, of course, my mother. She told me how she got up, wrapped a blanket around her, wrapped me in a raggedy towel, and then proceeded to walk toward the nearby river with its murky waters embraced by the long bamboo stalks waving eerily in the dark, still night.

It has always been on my mind—what was an incoherent woman whom had recently given birth doing on the road toward the river, in the middle of the night, still bleeding and with a little girl in her arms? Only God knows. Divine intervention played a great and miraculous part upon my birth. Was she going to dump me by the riverside so that I would never be seen again? Or was she taking herself to a neighbor in order to ask for help? Was she planning to walk the unimaginable long trek of miles in order to take me to my father's family house or perhaps to my father's house? So many questions that I had to tangle with and process as a child…those messages are long forgotten, the words and their meaning, the actions of a long-suffering woman. Was I to become a sacrificial offering to some unknown god or deity? What was going through her mind at that specific moment of my birth and the subsequent minutes and hours? I often wondered as a child what her intentions were then, but you know what? It does not matter now. I am here, and that is what matters the most. I made it. God provided a messenger. During my mother's long journey into the night, child in her arms, and maybe tears flowing down her face, she met the local midwife who had received the message of the coming birth and was on her way to my mom's house to assist her. According to my mom's recollection, the midwife, Dona Francisca, told my mother to turn back because it was dark, she had recently given birth, and she and the baby needed attention. My mom turned over the baby to the midwife and leaned against her, while trying to dry the mixture of watery blood that kept running down her legs. They walked along the dark, twisting rocky road back to her house, the dust clinging to their naked feet just as I was clinging to life in the midwife's arms. ..Only time will tell.

Chapter 3

Under the Shadow of the Mango Tree

It was either 1957 or 1958, my memory of the years fails me, but it was the time that the building of the Caserio Padre Nazario commenced. It was being built on the main road passing through the town of Guayanilla, and it was supposed to be the playground of the rich and famous, the working class of the town and neighboring localities. The vast fields of sugar cane were being razed, cut, and burned to make way for the next housing project. It was being built next to the local restaurant whose specialty included the scrumptious roast pork that was cooked on a stick over hot coals and tendered by the cook's assistant for many hours. Since it was located on the main road leading to and from town, many travelers, tourists, and locals stopped by this eatery to satiate their hunger and quench their thirst. Across the restaurant we could find the only gas station in town, which belonged to a man named Reynaldo and his sons.

The mountains of dark, rough sand and grey rocky gravel, along with mountains of yellow sulfur were seen from afar. The hustle and bustle of the many trucks carrying building supplies and materials were seen every day and left mountains of dust dancing in the air in the long, hazy island summer. Automobiles full of daily laborers would come and go, and the early morning doldrums of building, measuring, mixing, and carrying materials all over the construction site would begin.

We were dirt poor, and usually the task of getting at least dinner was not an easy one. Mom was a "Jill of all trades" who worked as a seamstress, made all kinds of crafts, made mountains of dry wood, dirt, and leaves in order to sell the burnt residue or coal, and begged for money dressed in the colors of the "saint of the day" or her favorite saints…she called it "keeping a promise made to the saints or the Virgin

Mary" and would take us along with her to the oil refinery in nearby Ponce…sometimes if she did not have the five cents to pay for public transportation, we would walk the ten or fifteen miles to get to the refinery. She also worked as a cook in the local roasted pork restaurant.

My mom's beau, named Jose Angel, used to slaughter the pigs and was also the "pork roaster". I remember the shrieking cries and the incessant wiggling of the pigs as they tried to break free while they were being led to the enormous wooden platform that served as the slaughterhouse. It was as if they knew their sad fate and were asking for forgiveness and hopefully another year of life. Their legs were hog-tied and sometimes it took a few men along with mom to put the pig on the platform for the kill. The haunting shrieks could be heard for miles. It took a few stabs just below their mouth, at the jugular, to put an end to their suffering and shrieks and complete the kill. Then, we, along with Mom, would bring pots of boiling water that was poured over the pig, and Jose Angel would carefully use an old, sharp, rusty blade to scrape the hair off the pig.

Mom readily assisted him in the slaughter, collected the blood, intestines and innards in order to make the blood pudding, and she would send us to the river to wash the intestines with a blue lime soap. I always wondered how in heavens we managed to balance aluminum tins and tubs full of intestines held only by a rolled, soiled towel on our little heads. Sometimes it would take my sisters and me hours just to wash a tub full of intestines, but we loved to swim in the river and search for water shrimp under the rocks. If Mom had to come and search for us at the river we would certainly get a beating, but it was worth it every effort to be able to take a dip in the cool, winding, refreshing waters in the river on those hot summer days.

Our reward after a hard day of work cleaning, washing, and drying pig intestines was delicious roasted pig feet, which we gnawed on for hours on end, and we never cared if our hands and mouths were sticky and smelly from the spices used to flavor the pig. For hungry children whose main interest was finding something to eat before nightfall, that was certainly a treat. Like hungry dogs, we would fight anyone who tried to take those roasted pig feet from us.

For many days since I was not school age anyway, I would take that long, lonely, dangerous trek across the grown cane fields to help in any way I could. Like a hungry puppy, I would wait impatiently for my treat.

In those days, finding food and not going to bed hungry at night took tremendous effort and survival skills, and I consider myself a survivor. While building the housing project, many of the neighborhood youth and children would lie hidden during the night in order to steal any material or tools they could find to sell at the plaza or to anyone willing to pay the asking price. So, the architect and building company in charge of the project decided to hire a night watchman to prevent looting and stealing. They brought a single wide metal trailer and put in the property right next to the rundown, leaning, one bedroom shack. We built this shack out of sheer necessity, and my mom was taken to court for being a squatter. She got off with a fine that, of course, she never paid.

This shack was built by my mom right under the old, gnarled mango tree that provided shade and fruits for the old lady Mercedes and our family that took shelter under its aged branches and knobby, contorted, venerable roots. Under the mango tree we built our old hut piece by piece. We used scrap wood, old metal signs for Shell Gas, KLIM milk and Winston cigarettes, and any other materials available and whatever else we could find. We had to scramble for metal buckets and small, empty tin containers every time it rained. We would huddle in a little corner, tired and shivering in that cold, leaky shack and pray for sunshine. The night watchman took residence in the single wide next to the shack under the mango tree, and my life was never the same.

Juaco, as everyone called him, was a tall, skinny man in his late thirties or early forties who was hired as the night security guard to safeguard the property and the materials. He was single, or so it appeared to us, but on his days off he would stand by the side of the road to either hitch a ride or take public transportation to some unknown location. We never knew if he had a wife or children or a family, but he must have had a family because his weekly trips soon became routine. He kept his hair cropped very short to the point of being bald, and he had a menacing way about him. He was also a stutterer, and the older children used to make fun of him. He was also very likable. The older children paid attention to his advice, but he was also a no-nonsense kind of guy who made sure everything was in order during the night.

He slept most of the day. Since he was a salaried employee, he was able to buy groceries, and being a single man, he shared his food with mom and us. Food!!! Such a wonderful, sweet, empowering word for a single mother and her little charges that were always so hungry. Food was scarce; jobs were nonexistent for a single woman with no skills and a bunch of shoeless, hungry kids with snotty noses and sticky faces. Yes! Those years were hard, and being able to eat was a precious commodity.

Juaco probably asked my mom to send me to get the daily portion of the food that he prepared because somehow I was the only one that went to his trailer in the afternoon, or maybe it was the fact that I was not school age, had no homework to complete, or had no other jobs like my older sisters. My younger sisters were either too young or mom felt that they would walk toward the main road, but I was "it".

He had all the possessions that attracted little children. I was born with an innate love for reading and was usually found huddled in a corner with a book or newspaper at hand immersed in my make-believe fantasy world of fairy tales and faraway lands. I think that I probably taught myself to read, as I remember waiting by the shack door for my brother and sisters to come home from school so that I can peruse their school books. I also went across the street to ask our kind and white haired neighbor Ms. Victoria for any old newspapers for my mother's art and crafts, and I would sit down for hours reading the paper and of course my favorites, Little Orphan Annie, Dagwood, The Phantom, Terry and the Pirates, Nancy, Little Lulu, Mandrake, Winnie Winkle, Dick Tracy, Prince Valiant, and so many other funnies!

Juaco had them all! He had all the comic books that a child could ever want. He had books with pictures. He had the novels that were my passion. He had bags and bags of candies. He had juices, sodas, pastries, cookies, cakes…anything and everything that a hungry, lonely, quiet, and reserved young child could ever want…and I had everything that a pedophile needed.

The first thing that Juaco did as soon as I came through that door was lock the door and the hatches. He was very kind, accommodating, friendly and all smiles at the beginning of the abuse. He would ask me if I wanted candy or food, and of course I said yes! After feeding my hunger, he would feed my eyes with books, comics, newspapers, etc., and any other things that I wanted. I remember feeling very uncomfortable as I saw that latch being locked and wondered countless times as to reasons for the door being locked.

He would sit close to me and caress my uncombed, curly, frizzy hair and massage my shoulders and would call me beautiful...me! A gawky, shoeless, skinny child who was always dressed in torn, dirty soiled clothes or hand-me-downs and who rarely used underwear because that was considered a luxury. I really don't remember how long it took Juaco to work his way up to full sexual intercourse, but I do clearly remember that I was not more than five or six years old at the time. The first time he penetrated me he put his hand over my mouth so the people outside would not hear my screams, my muffled cries, and his shrieks of delight.

It became an almost daily ritual. He would undress me, and I felt so uncomfortable lying in that thin, smelly mattress gazing at the ceiling and wondering how much longer I had until he unlatched the door. Usually, I practically ran out, exiting for my life, nervous, heart pounding,   embarrassed, ashamed at what was being done to me and carrying a heavy plate brimming with food in my hands.

The heat inside the trailer was unbearable and the hummm, thwack, hummm, thwack, hummm, thwack of the old rickety fan as it circulated the stale, hot air in that metal trailer reverberates in my ears to this date. The frayed electrical cord was held together by old black tape coming apart at the edges. The monotonous sounds helped me concentrate on getting out, escaping my tormentor, and thinking that soon the abuse would start all over again.

Many times, Juaco put my trembling, skinny, bony hands on his dark, erect, and warm penis and asked me to move my hand up and down, up and down, up and down, until whitish, sticky, reeking, foul-smelling semen inundated my hands; however, the worst was when he asked me to run my tongue over it, lick it, and swallow. He held my hands and would hold my throat until it was all gone. Other times, he would put his foul, uncircumcised penis in my mouth and would climax inside my mouth—such a sick feeling. Most of the times I gagged, become nauseous, and vomited right in the bed. I guess he was making sure that I was aware that he knew all the tricks of the pedophile trade as sometimes he would undress me completely, and his slimy, slithering, repulsive tongue would move up and down my whole body and orifices, leaving a sticky trail while I would just lay there quietly, in a catatonic state while taking glances at the locked door and wondering if anyone would come and knock loudly and maybe end my torment. Other times, the man just looked at me while he masturbated while standing next to the bed.

My only thoughts during those times were the fact that I needed to get out, the door was locked, and the musty, sweaty smell of the man permeated the whole house. I was also continually thinking that if I ran out I was going to trip over the mountains of dirty mildewed blue security uniforms and the stacks of books and newspapers. Now that am older I think that Juaco carefully planned to block the escape route on purpose, and he knew that I was trapped. I remember pretending that I was sick so that I would not be sent any more to his trailer to collect food, but it rarely worked. I was available, we were a hungry family, and food was being sent home.

Mom would share the food that Juaco sent with my brother and sisters, but I never wanted to eat the food that he prepared. My mom would say, "Ungrateful child! Ungrateful child! The man is so kind that he is willing to share his food with us. Now sit down and eat your share or go to bed hungry!" Most times I chose to go to bed hungry because I knew the burning and the heartache, the shame that I always felt after the abuse and how many tears flowed from my little eyes as my innocence was being taken away again and again by the "kind man" named Juaco.

Every day or week or whatever time frame such a long time ago, that this abuse was taking place, I always wondered why, why my mother never checked on me or knocked on the door to see what was going on, why other adults gathered around under the mango tree, the other shacks, and the main house did not wonder why that little girl was spending so much time locked in a trailer with an older man. Where were my older brother and sisters during this time; were they working? Studying? Did anyone care enough to check on an innocent, little girl who was being preyed upon?

WHY? I guess I will never have the answer to my questions, and at this point the questions no longer matter to me. What matters is that I was strong and resilient and survived one of the darkest chapters of my life.

There were many wooden shacks built by the sons of Mercedes, who lived in the main house. Her sons later moved to the United States, and she succumbed into her own little world. Mercedes was a kind, dark, wrinkly old lady who was supposed to be a relative of my mom. She was a sweetheart, but she lived in her own fantasy world of remembrances. A time long gone she used to chew tobacco, and her tongue was as black as a night without stars. She was always spitting dark, sticky, fetid saliva, and she used to drink homemade moonshine, which was delivered by one of her cronies on a weekly basis. She used to guard that moonshine as if it was a treasured possession.

No one could explain what was wrong with her, but thinking back now I am certain she had Alzheimer's disease. She lived alone, and my mother as well as her daughter, Edith, and her son, Polo, would check on her occasionally. Polo and Edith at one time moved away to the states but came back and lived elsewhere. I always thought that Edith was a prostitute and Polo was a jailbird. I know for a fact that Polo was a jailbird because once, as we were gathered under the mango tree, a police car stopped in front of Mercedes house, went inside and took a handcuffed Polo outside, put him inside the squad car, and drove away. Edith used to stand by the side of the road wearing the shortest shorts I had ever seen and tons of make up or a tight tube mini-dress, stopping cars driving along the main road. Many times I saw her getting inside cars driven by single men, and they readily sped away. One day I went inside the house looking for Mercedes and came upon Edith and a man in a very compromising position. The man had his hand down Edith's short pants, and with his other hand he held her breast and was sucking on her nipple. They were so surprised! In the blink of an eye and in the shortest split second possible, they disengaged, put a halt to their amorous activity, and shooed me away, the man cursing at me under his breath. Sometimes, I still can hear Edith's cackling and echoing laughter as I ran away from the house.

Mercedes was very forgetful and would make pots of soup out of days old rice and red beans that had been in the sun or in her pantry for hours or maybe days. Who knows? None of my sisters of brother wanted to eat her pot of rancid, smelly soup, but I did; hunger does not discriminate! Oh, how they used to make fun of me for eating Mercedes' concoctions and putrid experiments, but I didn't mind; it filled my stomach and stopped the hunger pangs.

She also taught me how to play brisca or the Tarot cards used to tell the fortune. I was smart as a whip, and after a while I used to win all the games, or maybe in her kindness she let me win.

Poor Mercedes! I remember her being locked in her house by her son and daughter and her trying to climb out the window and ripping her old, saggy, sun-weathered, leathery skin in the process. Many times she got lost by the construction site or the river and some poor soul brought her back home to be locked again. She would be brought back to her house, and sometimes she was full of thorns, a bloody mess, lumps and scratches all over her face and her head while she tried to run away and probably fell. She was a kindred spirit, poor Mercedes.

My mom and Mercedes used to cook for the laborers working in the construction site, and some of them rented the wooden shacks around Mercedes house. I imagine they lived in other towns, so it did not make sense for them to go back home after a hard day's work, or maybe they did not have a place to live. Then again, however, they gave Mercedes and my mom a small allowance for the "luxury" of a home cooked meal once in a while.

Again, it was my "job" to deliver the meals to the shacks and I did so faithfully without rebelling or questioning the motives because I knew that surviving those times depended mostly on my being compliant and that the measly stipend given to my mom would put food in the table and in my stomach.

Johnny or Juan, I cannot recall his real name or maybe he gave Mercedes a false name, rented one of the old wooden shacks from Mercedes, and I recall delivering food to him on an almost daily basis. He was a short stocky black man who appeared to be in his late thirties or early forties with slicked back, greasy black hair that was probably straightened with a mixture of lye and potatoes, which was very popular in those days. His putrid breath smelled of cigarette smoke and old tobacco and his teeth, or the ones that he still had were rotten, decayed, black, and stained yellow from countless years of smoking those hand-rolled, no brand cigarettes. He had rheumy, evil, old eyes that squinted continually as if trying to get rid of a headache or trying to erase the haziness of his life.

And every time that I delivered his food he took liberties with me. He would put his stinking, slimy, rancid tongue inside my mouth, and he would wiggle his tongue, French-kissing me and getting angry because I would not respond to his freaky advances. While exploring my mouth and my lips with his filthy tongue, he would fondle me with his dirty hands and fingers me while at the same time making the most lewd movements and uttering obscene words that burned my ears and brought tears to my eyes. After a while, contributing to my sake and sanity, Johnny moved away, and I never heard from or saw him again.

Don Miguel was a friend of Mom and Mercedes. He lived on the "other side of the tracks," or the good part of town. He was at least seventy years old, and his weekly afternoon visits to Mercedes were very well received by the children in the neighborhood because of the gifts of fruits and candy that he always brought with him. He had some problems with his leg and always used a beautiful ebony cane topped by what appeared to a small golden bird. He was so proud of that cane! He was probably myopic as evidenced by the thick, black-rimmed, bottleneck glasses he wore with pride. He always dressed meticulously in a while linen suit or a white guayabera with white linen pants. His clothes were always so clean that they appeared to shine when the sunlight was reflected on the threads. His straw hat was always a perfect fit, and he wore it like it was a royal crown. He had poise and character, and it was obvious that he lived an affluent life and that he liked little girls, but his philanthropic ways took a different turn with me.

One day he came to visit, a strange visit because it was midday, the kids were at school, Mom was somewhere at work, and Mercedes was on her merry way trying to escape through the raggedy old window framed by metal signs. I was not in school and was inside our wooden shack babysitting my baby sister when out of the blue I heard the creaking sound of the door opening. There was Don Miguel in all the splendor of his white suit and straw hat leaning on his beautiful cane with a small brown paper bag filled with penny candy in his other hand. Don Miguel tried to engage me in chitchat, asking about mom, her whereabouts, my sisters, and the reason for me being left alone at the house with my baby sister. While he was busily engaged in his line of questioning, I was pretty sure that by this time Mercedes was happily laughing on her way to the river or some unknown place that was known only by her lonely and pitiful soul.

Don Miguel sat in the only wobbly wooden chair available and asked me to come over to pick some candy from the small brown bag. As I got closer, he grabbed me with all his strength, and the gorgeous ebony cane hit the floor with such force that I thought it had broken in many parts. I struggled with Don Miguel as he tried to put his hand under my dress and hold my hands at the same time. Both of us were trembling and sweating as one struggled to get his way and I struggled for my life. At that time, I forgot about my baby sister and pushed Don Miguel so hard that he fell backwards, chair on top of him, ebony cane to one side, black-rimmed glasses to the other, his white hair damped with the sweat of the struggle while my heart pounded as I tried to catch my breath during the struggle to break free. On all fours, I crawled all the way to the door to break free. I ran for what it seemed like an eternity and hid in the woods while Don Miguel, in his unsuccessful, dazed stupor, limped all the way to his house on the good side of town.

It happened one of those days as I was working my way through the sugar cane fields engrossed in my thoughts about the succulent treat of roasted pig feet waiting for me at the restaurant. There was a cool breeze dancing among the rows upon rows of cane fields that seemed to embrace the long, leggy stalks of the sugar cane plants, and the sugar cane flowers in return gave off the sweet smell of burnt sugar as they were caressed by the breeze. Once in a while I stopped to listen to the croaky tunes hummed by the bullfrogs, as they tried to entertain a nearby toad, saw the fluttery dance of the colorful monarch butterflies as they scurried along busily looking for a wildflower from which to extract nectar and the slow pace of an occasional black, yellow and orange furry caterpillar as it crawled leisurely toward the fields. I was always scared to death of anything that crawled, and the caterpillars were no exception, but being the free- spirited child that I was who loved nature and its wonders, I would grab a stick and sit in front of the creepy crawler just to block its path and see how it rolled itself into a colorful circle and, once it knew that the coast was clear, continue on its busy path ahead.

Suddenly, and without making a sound, which was very surprising since when you walk in the sugar cane fields, every leaf, every stalk, every plant will block your path and anyone nearby can tell that you are coming, the old man must who had been waiting was crouched, stalking for his next victim. I had not heard a sound and all of a sudden I saw a pair of old, worn, leather shoes right next to me only to look up to see this old man with dirty, torn, raggedy clothes and a lusty look on his unshaven, stubby face. His voice was hoarse as he tried to whisper to tell me not to move.

My heart was pounding as I heard that voice, and all of a sudden, the sound made by the wind as it traveled from stalk to stalk was magnified about a hundred times. The panic that I felt at the time cannot be described here, but I felt cold, giant drops of perspiration running down my face, a bitter knot traveled from my stomach to my throat, and I felt as if I was choking. My hands and my legs became paralyzed and would not respond to my weak command to drop everything and run for my life. The knot in my throat would not let my feeble screams become known. Finally, I felt the burning path of my hot urine as it exited my body, traveling down my legs and settling in a muddy puddle as it mixed with the damp earth. I just stood there like a salt statue with eyes as big as saucers as my heart pounded stronger and stronger and a thousand thoughts sped through my mind.

I was paralyzed with fear but was able to see the man lower his zipper and expose his fully erect penis while he tried to grab me all at the same time. It happened in a split second—the sound of the wind, the chirping of the birds, the earthly smells—and I was just standing there, as if someone had just dug a hole and planted my feet deeply in the ground and an unknown force was holding me down. My legs were like jellyfish, moving, but at the same time not going anywhere. My screams would not come out as if there was no one around to hear my silent, desperate cries for help; they refused to make their exit. My whole body was not responding with the exception of my eyes, which kept looking from side to side as if searching for a quick escape route, searching for help, searching for the help that I knew would never come because the sugar cane fields were no place for little children or for little girls walking alone. In my mind I saw giant tentacles rising from the damp earth and engulfing my shaky, bony, trembling legs, my wobbly knees, my waist, my shivering hands and arms, finally wrapping those thin, powerful knotted cords around my pulsating, throbbing neck, trying to suffocate me, trying to extract every living breath from my young and innocent soul.

Suddenly, however, an overpowering, unnatural strength surrounded me, the strength of an eagle flying up above the sky, flying to the air as if someone was trying to harm her young eaglets. I felt the tentacles giving way, becoming soft and being swallowed by the earth that seemed to shake as I crawled on all fours, panting, sweating, tears mixed with dirt rolling down my face, my dirty, raggedy clothes getting torn by the overgrown underbrush while I felt the stinging, scraping injuries of the silt, the gravel, and the dirt as they scraped my hands, my face, and my knees.

But I ran fast like a wounded doe, like a wild palomino horse in the western fields, eyes wide open, looking for a way out, searching frantically for that inviting opening in the fertile cane fields, the blades of the green, knobby stalks hitting my face and wounding my skin as I flew like a bird, at times feeling as if my feet were off the ground, the sweltering air trying to exit my lungs and burning my nostrils in the process.

While running, the sensation of invisible, powerful hands carrying me across the fields was so powerful and overwhelming, while at the same time, I desperately glanced back over my shoulder, just to see a struggling, masculine figure that seemed to appear smaller and smaller as I gained distance. In an instant, I disappeared among the cane fields, panting, crying, falling, getting up, stepping on unknown, squishy creatures until I reached safety in the grounds of my favorite restaurant whose specialty was roasted pork and in the arms of my mom, who was busy preparing lunch, only to be scolded, spanked, and hit by Jose Angel's large, leathery belt, which she folded in two so that it would double the pain. I was punished for coming to the roadside eatery during its most busy lunch stretch looking like a poor soul that had not bathed in years and for leaving my little sister alone.

Again, there were no questions, no kind loving words, no explanations asked, no loving embrace or the soft caress of a motherly hand trying to clean a child's dirty face or unkempt hair, just the sad, lingering, suffering, invisible pain and the stinging, aching agony of the cuts and bruises inflicted by the sugar cane stalks as the dark red blood oozed and stuck to the wounds.

I never ventured through the cane fields by myself again and I never saw that ugly, evil force of a man ever again, but even today, as an adult, I still look over my shoulder just to make sure that I am safe—just to make sure.

I was sent back home, but this time I took the main

road, where I hoped that at least someone would stop to

help if by an unfortunate turn of events the ogre decided to

stalk me again, walking slowly and painfully with a

wounded, suffering soul along the edge of the road. The

soft murmurs of the tropical winds and the vroom, vroom

of the motors of the occasional cars as they sped along the

long, winding, desolate road were my only comfort during

the quiet trip back, while the laughter of children walking

home from school echoed through my ears and thoughts of

a brighter future filled my lonely heart.

Don Eloy, as everyone called him was an angel, a

pitiful, twisted shape of a man whose dreams seemed to

have been shattered eons ago, but his soul was as beautiful

and clear as the rushing waters of a waterfall, and he was a

God-given gift to the little children dreaming of far away,

enchanted and mysterious lands. He had been born with

what   appeared   to   be

cerebral palsy and also had some speech delays. His hands were dark and aged, and the protruding veins spoke of years of strain and pain. He was maybe eighty or ninety years old, dark as the night; the only teeth in his mouth were stained yellow and black maybe from being unable to brush them due to his handicap or the misfortunes of being born poor. Don Eloy had never been married and lived alone in a little wooden one-room house about a mile from our shack.

He had a little, homemade wooden cart that resembled a wheelbarrow with uneven long pieces of wood for walls and an old, wooden leaky roof. He carried his wooden carvings of saints, animals, and crosses in his little cart and would trudge about town trying to sell his wares. He was such a good soul! And he was also a very happy man, or so he seemed to me. I never heard Don Eloy complain of his misery, his life, his loneliness, or his livelihood.

Every afternoon, once the sun began to settle in the horizon and the shadows of the leafy twisted branches of the old mango tree began to dance their nocturnal dance on our dirt patio, and as the family gathered sitting in whatever rocks we could find, we would see the slow, excruciating shuffle of Don Eloy as he walked down the path to Mercedes house to eat his measly portion of whatever food or leftovers were available or Mercedes' daily flavorless concoctions to be topped off by a cup of my mom or Mercedes' black, strong bitter homemade coffee.

Apparently, Don Eloy never changed his clothes, and he always wore the same dark, stained pants held up by a piece of dirty rope, a grayish shirt that was supposed to be white but changed color after many years of being worn and not washed, a heavy woolen, soiled jacket with missing buttons, and a khaki dirty overcoat. This not-so GQ combination was worn by Don Eloy even during the most incessantly hot days of the summer on the island. It was a known fact by everyone concerned, including the adults and the children that Don Eloy never changed nor washed his clothes or his undergarments. I imagined that due to his handicapping condition, he was not able to change his clothes and maybe slept in them due to their disheveled, craggy, and wrinkled appearance. He certainly did not smell like an "angel," and the stench of urine and dried feces could be whiffed for miles away, but the children didn't care about Don Eloy's smell or appearance.

The children would gather around Don Eloy, and to him this was the highlight of his arduous day. He came to Mercedes' house every evening, not for the daily ration of nutritional sustenance, but for his daily allotment of children's laughter, giggles, and the magic touch of the children's hands as we lovingly held his calloused hands and guided him to his favorite chair. He performed magic tricks to the oohs and ahhs of the little ones, and his twisted mouth grunted the most wonderful sound effects heard by little ears! We were enthralled and captivated by his million and one stories, and our imaginations were transported instantly to magical lands. Now as I think back about our beloved Don Eloy, I think that God gave him the special gift of bringing laughter and a sparkle to children's' eyes. I am pretty sure, as I write this story, that Don Eloy was the male version of Scheherazade, making up stories night after night to mesmerize not the Persian king, but the little children that brought so much meaning to his life. I don't know how and when Don Eloy departed this earthly world, but I know for sure that he is now entertaining little angels up in heaven and that the love for stories that he instilled in a little lonely girl decades ago still lives.

I always heard my mother's comments that I had been a child born out of rape when she had been separated from my father and lived alone in Los Indios, another ward about twenty-five miles north of the wooden shack. She was fifteen when she went to live with my father, Fito, who was twenty-five years her senior. By the time she was eighteen, she had three boys, Junior, Oscar, and Jose B., who were taken away from her and raised by my paternal aunt Adela. After her children were taken away, my mom had other children from different men, ran away to San Juan, came back, and tried to make ends meet, but her older three boys were never returned to her. She used to say that once she came back from San Juan, she settled into a small rental house in Los Indios and would work in the glove making industry, sewing and making fancy needlework designs on the gloves.

One night, and according to my mother's recollections, after putting my brother and sisters to sleep, my alcoholic father came to the house, pulled a gun out of his waist, and forced my mother to have sex with him. Nine months later and in the same house, I made my grand entrance into this world.

After my birth, my mother and father never lived together as a couple under one roof, but he would come to see me and take me to his sister's house so that my older brothers could meet and play with me. Afterwards, my mother moved out of the house and took her children to live in the shack built by her under the shadows of the mango tree.

My father would pedal on his old, colorful bike for miles to come and see me. Though he drank alcohol and moonshine all his life, he always managed to hold a job as a laborer in the sugar cane fields. The two measly dollars he gave my mother as a form of child support helped put food in our mouths, but being a laborer in the sugar cane fields was only temporary employment since most laborers were unemployed once the sugar cane harvesting season was over. And weeks and months would come and go before my mom saw another two dollars. But his weekly visits to see his daughter never stopped. He would travel on his bike. All the neighboring children knew that my father would come on Sundays, and they would gather to hop in the bike and get rides through the main road to the bridge overlooking the Guayanilla River and back. Since I was his little girl, he would pedal double the distance when he would pick me up and put me on his bike.

Also, I guess since my mom had too many children and it was so difficult for her to keep watch over them, she would let me spend the weekends with my father, a single, alcoholic man who lived alone in a house in Los Indios. He would bathe me, comb my hair, prepare coffee, and would take me to his sister's house to get food. At nightfall, he would carry me to the house and lay me down in the old, creaky metal bed next to him. One day I saw the gun under the pillow.

I am not trying to make excuses for my father and for many years I tried to understand the sexual abuse from numerous perpetrators I encountered as a child, but I am still trying to come to grips or understand the things done to me by someone who professed to love me, whose eyes shone like the sun upon seeing me, by someone whom was instrumental in giving me life and bringing me into this world.

Yes, I was a victim of incest. It is one of the most horrible forms of abuse. I not trying to diminish the previous sexual, emotional and physical abuse encountered as a child, but how do you deal with the atrocious and hideous act of incest committed by someone that you loved and trusted? Will I ever come to grips with the fact that my father used to have sex with his little girl and that he was a pedophile? From where, Lord oh Lord, do I gain the strength to dissipate those images, acts, and thoughts from my very being?

I remember him coming to see me or the family during those days as a child. One day, I was sitting next to him eating the candies that he had brought, and he picked up my baby sister who was about two at the time. His big hand started moving first up my sister's leg, up to her thighs, and slowly but oh! So slowly his hand finally went up my little sister's underwear and found what apparently he was looking for and gave him satisfaction. Out of the corner of my eye, in a fleeting instant and in disbelief, unable to speak in protest of what was being done to my baby sister, angry at myself at my inability to protect her and angry at my father for destroying another little girl's innocence, I continued to watch as my father's long middle finger moved in and out, in and out, in and out of my little sister's vagina and silent tears started to come down my face.

To this day I ask myself, Lord, why did I let it happen? Where were my screams and my cries of protest? Was it because at the tender age of six I had nothing else to give or no hopes of being rescued? If I was going to be able to make a difference and save a little girl, where was my strength and my anger when I needed it the most? Why did I let my little sister down and allow the abuse to continue? Would it have made a difference if I told an adult what was being done to me and my sister? I guess not. I felt hopeless, trapped. Life had been sucked out of me like an exhaust fan, and the fumes of fury were being dispersed into the silent wind. During those times I felt trapped, alone. There were no adults to hear my cries, to rescue me from the depravation and evil around me, no one to assist, nobody to hear my silent outcries, or to dry my tears, which continued to leave unseen emotional pathways around my long-suffering, beating heart.

Under the shade of the magnanimous mango tree I learned the value of the money earned during a hard day's work. I guess that I started my unpaid employment, or better yet my first job whose fringe benefits included timidly coming home with a plate of food in my hand and with my heart pumping like a giant machine, readily dashing to the protection of the leaning wooden shack trying to avoid another embarrassing ass whooping. The real motivation, however, was trying to hide the embarrassment and the heaviness of the invisible mark of Cain felt deep within my heart and which I was pretty sure was readily evident on my forehead.

My older sisters found work cleaning the mansions of the affluent ladies and widows who lived around the plaza and in the street behind the Catholic Church. Some of the mansions were so huge that I always wondered why the ladies lived there alone while we had to live in a rundown, homemade wooden shack. These were mansions with iron fences and gates everywhere in order to keep the less fortunate out, but I guess that the poor widows were the real prisoners there. They had huge, Moroccan style wraparound porches with inlaid Italian and Spanish tiles in beautiful designs.

My sister's jobs included going around the rooms to make up beds that had not provided a restful sleep to a tired visitor in years, dusting the same objects d'art, antique tables, and furniture day after boring day, filling the colorful, glass blown vases with fresh picked flowers from the beautiful gardens, and making sure that the ladies' garments were washed, ironed, dried, and hung in the huge chifforobes.

I loved going to work with my sisters. Sometimes, while helping with selecting the flowers, I would scurry, hopefully unnoticed, glancing back and from side to side, looking at the fancy, ornate grillwork of the windows facing the gardens to ensure that there was not a set of old, squinty eyes following my every move as I silently made my way to the back of the gardens. It was there that the mango trees, brimming with the splendor of their delicious fruit, would stoop down, tired from the fruity heaviness and willing to give their precious possessions back to the earth or to the little deprived girl who visited almost daily to scoop the fresh mango fruits and put them in a brown paper bag where they were hidden in the flower garden like the most exquisite, delightful gifts from nature.

And back to work I went, going from room to room, scooping up the white, stained enameled pissing pots to take them outside to be scrubbed with a mixture of Clorox and other chemicals until my nails and fingers felt raw to the bone, reddish and hurting. I still remember the stench of the urine and the mixture of chemicals going down my throat and settling in my stomach until a gagging, nauseated feeling permeated my intestines and bones, my spirit and my soul. When it was over at the end of the week, on Friday evenings, the ladies would give my older two sisters fifteen cents to be divided among them. For me, well, I would sit quietly, trying not to notice my dirty feet and inflamed small hands as the enormous, carved wooden door opened and a gloved hand placed two pennies on the outside only to be quickly closed again. Those two pennies were readily scooped up. In a split second, the treasured bag full of mangoes lying hidden in the garden, was also gathered up while frizzy hairs flew in unison as I ran back home, proud of my work and ready to place two dirty, sticky old pennies in my mother's hands. I was so proud that I was able to contribute to the family's finances! I must have been probably five or six years old when I started to clean and disinfect enameled pissing pots, but the skills and the experiences acquired during those first jobs taught me invaluable lessons during my formative years.

Another time, the elementary school concierge named Concha hired my brother to be her assistant. Ms. Concha was an older, stocky, olive-skinned lady in her fifties who had been working at the school for years. She was probably tired of cleaning, of working, of life in general when she hired my older brother Edwin to help her with cleaning the school, outside property, and rooms. Of course, my brother, astute as he was, hired my sister Betty and me to do his job. We cleaned the blackboards, swept and mopped the floors and the long, tiled hallways, took the erasers outside to bang them against each other to get all the white chalky residue out, cleaned out the desks, emptied out the trash cans, and took bags of green garbage bags out. We did all the work while Ms. Concha would go to the principal's office, lock the door, and read the daily paper or magazines and my brother Edwin would go to another empty classroom to read comic books.

Fridays was one of the sweetest days for us…payday!!!   Concha would give my brother two old, wrinkled dollars, and he would give us a quarter each! Talk about a promotion…from the measly two cents to twenty-five cents all for me!! During those times when a pound of rice was sold for five cents and you could also buy two cents' worth of lard, two cents of sugar and three cents for a pound of beans, a quarter seemed like so much money! As always, I ran home to place that quarter in my mother's hand, but I knew that Sunday was just right around the corner and on Sundays, my brother would treat us to the movies—the weekly newscasts, the funnies, the western series, and finally the movie!!! And Mom would give me enough to buy penny candy. You see, life under the shade of the huge mango tree was not always depressing, abusive, or sad. Life for me growing up in a homemade wooden shack built under the embracing, enormous branches of that beautiful, aged, tired mango tree had its beautiful moments.

Ahhh!!If only the mango tree could speak! It would tell tales of children running and playing in its branches, of evening stories by adults sitting around a campfire, and mesmerized children fighting Morpheus' embrace while swatting mosquitoes and trying to imprison the beautiful and elusive lightning bug. The old, gnarled, wise tree would tell of its insides about to burst when feeling the symbiotic energy from the forceful push and monotonous drone of homemade swings, of old, ragged tires held together by jagged ropes discarded by old sailors. It would tell stories of children squealing with delight as the old swings and tires seemed to point and fly toward the invisible horizons and the blue hazy sky, and little trapeze artists, feeling the boundless energy leaving their bodies after countless hours of climbing strong tree branches and swinging aimlessly under the silent, watchful eyes of the aged mango tree.

I always thought that I could hear the silent, satisfied chuckle of my mango tree, as tired, listless, dirty, and sweaty children paraded silently in their daily shuffle toward the inside of the old, rickety wooden shack.

Chapter 4

8-12

After living under the shade of the old mango tree,
we finally were able to rent a house in another ward called
Magas Abajo. We rented a big, lovely house with an
outdoor latrine, three bedrooms, living room, kitchen, and
dining area; it was enormous! Plus it was fenced in! It had
been built on the top of a rocky mountain, right in front of
another big tree, the bucida buceras, better known as the
Ucar tree, and characterized by its thick green foliage. It
grows on dry terrain and is very common in the islands,
often used for landscaping and greenery. I would sit by the
porch just to reminisce and enjoy the fresh, mountain air,
which smelled like damp dirt, rain, and wildflowers. It was
a majestic view. If you looked closely you could see the
main road, the valley, and the muddy waters of the river
meandering its way toward the bay. The view from the
porch was just stunning until the torrential rains came

down! The house was situated on the hilly side of the rocky mountain, and when it rained, the path to go down the main road became as slippery as an eel. If you decided to go down you had to hold on to the wooden or chicken wire fences for dear life; otherwise, you became part of the load being carried away by the forceful rains.

Our house was the third one from the top, and our neighbors were Chofe and Maria Luisa and their twelve children. Right next to them were Adrian and Gladys, who had four children, one of them autistic. Right next to Gladys lived Quirito, a sweet hydrocephalic teenage boy who was not supposed to live past six but who somehow beat the odds. And last but not least was my friend Pascuala, or Coa as everyone called her, my protector, my mentor, my friend, and a loving woman whom I still remember for her kindness and the joy that she projected despite being a victim of domestic violence. Her husband Toño was supposed to be my mother's distant relative. Going down the mountain and under the shade of the big Ucar three there lived Don Eusebio, his wife, Doña Marias, and their children, Mingo and Brenda. Mingo was a college student, involved in the independence movement, and believed by many to be a member of the Macheteros or the "Machete Wielders". Years later, we found out that Mingo had been arrested for murder. I thought that there was something wrong with Brenda. She was sixteen years old and did not attend school. Her face and her back were scarred by acne, but she was also the champion when it came to playing a game of jacks.

Maria Luisa and her children used to run an illegal casino, or so we thought because we would scramble looking for money to go to her house to play lotto. We would bet from one to six cents, and if Maria Luisa and her ten older children played, the pot would be sweetened based on the number of players. But they cheated through their teeth!! And they always won the pot. I think they marked the cardboard lotto cards or read the wrong numbers, but they always won.

We were always scrambling, looking for someone to give us a morsel of food. I used to go the undeveloped part of the mountain to look for dry wood to bring to Coa so she could cook. She also lived in a small, two-bedroom wooden house, and her kitchen was outside the house. She had a dirt floor, a little kerosene stove, and some pots and pans, and she needed the wood for cooking so that the little gallon of kerosene would last longer. Coa fit the maxim "pregnant and barefooted" stereotype to a tee. She had a child every year. I always wondered how she managed to get pregnant because her husband Toño used to sleep in the full-size bed, which hardly fit in one of the rooms, and Coa and her eight children would sleep in cots or a little twin-size bed in the other room. Toño had a little candy stand in front of the movie house but also had a lover in another town. From the window of one of the rooms Coa could see if Toño was coming home. The food had better be ready, or there was going to be hell to pay. She also knew if Toño was drunk as a skunk and would tell the children and me to scramble. Coa was a wonderful cook, and I still can taste her daily fare of green peas and white rice...poor thing! I don't think she had enough food for her husband, herself ,and her children, but she lovingly shared her ration of food with me and my sisters, who sometimes just happened to meander in just about supper time.

I would go inside the house to help sweep and mop the floors and bathe the children in tiny tin tubs filled with rainwater. After bathing the little ones, I would scrub their clothes in the same tub and put the clothes to dry on top of the bushes or the small tress growing on the edge of the mountain. I would take the dirty mats Coa and her children used to sleep in outside to make sure the bed bugs, dirt, and crumbs were swatted away. While doing chores in Coa's house, her older son, Wilmer, would fondle and grab me, would twist my small nipples, which were starting to form, would hold my arms behind my back and pinch me and would bite me so hard that at times I cringed and cried in pain. I never told my friend Coa, however, as I was afraid to hurt her feelings or of being told that I could not come back to the house and, in the process, lose my ration of her delicious food.

Don Eusebio and his family lived under the shade of the big Ucar tree in a big wooden house on stilts. He was a much hated man in the community, mostly by the children, and I can imagine why. He was a short, stooped, skinny, and tanned from years of working outside in the fields and around the house, gardening and tending to his vegetables and flowers.

He had little beady eyes that seemed to be in constant motion, on alert mode, looking from side to side, always looking for his next prey. With his misshapen head, with its patches of salt and pepper hair, he seemed to be plotting to pounce on his next victim. His leathery, toady skin looked as if it was be stuck to his protruding bones. His hooked nose resembled the beak of a black crow, and his shuffled gait was that of a wounded, vicious animal.

He was a repugnant, offensive, ugly, dirty old man, in total contrast to his dear old wife, Doña Maria, and he was a hated man. He would stand by the fence and expose himself to the children going down the rocky path or make obscene gestures with his hands, inviting little children to come inside toward the back of the house. Other times, he would masturbate in full view of the children, and he would scramble when rocks were thrown at him. He was a sick man, despised by many, especially by his own daughter, Brenda, who would scream and curse at him constantly. I wondered why, but when I became his victim of sexual abuse, it was easy to assume that he had also sexually abused his own daughter.

At the tender age of eight years old, Don Eusebio, the pederast, sexually abused me. It usually took place in one of the vacant bedrooms on the other side of the kitchen where his wife spent most of her time. Once the games of jacks with Brenda finished, she would get very tired, and she would retire to her own bedroom to sleep. I managed to hang around especially around dinner time to see if something happened to fall off the table, figuratively speaking, and of course, since their son, Mingo, was going to the university, there were always many books and magazines in the room, which attracted me to the room. The weasel would come in, have his way with me, and then go outside again, only to make more obscene gestures as I left his house and look around with his lusty, squinty eyes to see if anyone was looking at him.

One night, as people were making their way down the rocky alley to the main road and the town park to attend a religious procession, I stayed behind to take a sponge bath. There was no running water in our rented house. We either gathered rainwater or went down the hill to fill plastic pails and grudgingly brought them up the hill. I filled the rusty aluminum tin with water, gathered my clean clothes and a raggedy towel, and proceeded to bathe myself. After finishing my bird bath, as I was walking toward the other room and drying myself and while standing alone in the room completely naked and vulnerable, there stood this tall, black man by the door, looking at me and slowly walking toward me, carefully measuring his steps. I recognized him as a friend of my mom; he was a man named Grimales.

I ran outside, holding my clothes like a soul that has seen the red face of the devil, and hid under the house, heart pumping, adrenaline rushing, wet, damp skin gathering dirt in the process, but I did not care. I needed to get away! I stood under the house for what seemed like hours until I saw the dark, stumbling figure leave the house and go down the rocky hill toward the main road and the procession.

I waited until I could no longer see the lonely shadow disappearing in the night heat and ran to the porch where I glanced around to make sure there was no one coming down the hill to see my naked little body while I tried to put on my clothes. I ran all the way down to the main plaza and the procession, frizzy, damp curly hair dancing in the night wind while my heart kept pumping at least one hundred gallons of blood per split second, thoughts racing through my mind. I immediately glanced around and scanned the crowds, trying to make some sense of the of the shadowy, dancing figures holding lighted taper or beeswax candles, of plaster and wooden saints being carried on top of wooden platforms, of the colorful gowns and headgear worn by the procession participants, carefully looking for those familiar faces and a safe haven.

It was the summer of 1965, June 21st to be exact, when I first heard the news of my father's death. I was sitting on the porch of the rented house admiring the views and letting the fresh summer air caress my hair and my face when out of the corner of my eye I saw a lonely young man making his way up the hilly alleyway. My brother Jose had the saddest look on his face, came around, hugged my mom and told her the ill-fated news. While working in the muddy cane fields, my father had been injured when a razor-sharp, rusty machete nicked his leg. An infection developed, and by the time my father was taken to the hospital with a burning temperature, the infection had created havoc in his body and it was too late to save him. He died of tetanus that morning. I went to his funeral and his wake, but not his burial.

As I stood by myself looking at that golden casket and his lifeless, inert body lying peacefully in those silky white sheets, his stiff hands holding a golden rosary with a tiny crucifix, at the young, tender age of eleven, right then and there I made one of the most important decisions of my life. I decided that I was not going to hold on to his sin. I decided to forgive my father for what he had done to my little sister and me. I decided to go on with my life. I decided to forgive and not let the sins of my father take root in my heart, and I learned that forgiveness is the most powerful weapon given to man.

After the sudden death of my father, my mom decided that it was time for new beginnings, new horizons, a new take on life, and ordered us to pack up our paltry belongings so she could try to look for a job in the big city. The capital, with its hustle and bustle, the throngs of people, the drugs, the shanty towns and new experiences for little children from a small town in the southern part of the isle, was the big city she chose. We went to live with relatives during that summer while my mom moved to San Juan with the promise that once she secured housing and a job, she would come for us.

Chapter 5
Santurce and San Juan

My mom finally came to get us, and we moved to the bustling, busy town of Santurce, a town with many stores, colorful row houses, hectic lifestyles, and every imaginable sin. My mom was employed as a cook's helper in my uncle's mobile restaurant. His wife, Tia Isabel, a black matron who bossed everyone around, was the main cook. My mother would assist in the kitchen, helping load the dinner truck and going with my uncle to different construction sites to sell the delicious home cooked meals. We lived in a little room right next to the commercial kitchen that doubled as a warehouse and storage area for the many products used in the kitchen. There were no windows, so it was very dark. We would study and do our homework outside before the sun settled in the horizon and Mom almost went blind by sewing at night under the incandescent light of a small light bulb. The suffocating heat was unbearable, and the frequent smells and rancid odors emanating from the mixture of different spices, meats, fish and red, white and pink beans, garbanzo beans, cabbage, onions, garlic, and other greens was nauseating and unpleasant to the senses during our stay in this little, dark, oppressing room.

We were thankful that we had a roof over our heads. My mom had a job and she paid only a small fraction of her salary in rent. She supplemented her measly wages by sewing all kind of dresses, pants, uniforms and by selling arts and crafts and all kinds of beauty products, which we delivered to her clients during the afternoons and on weekends.

Oh! But what a culture shock, what a rude awakening for a bunch of little country girls! After a few months my uncle and Tia Isabel bought a brand new, beautiful house in a subdivision close to San Juan, and my mother rented the main house from them. It was a bright, colorful, spacious, and comfortable wooden house full of big windows, linoleum, and tiled floors. It had a side garden where we planted tomatoes, peppers, okra and eggplants. Best of all, it had an inside latrine and running water. Its big wooden slatted porch faced the busy avenue, and we would sit on the porch in the evenings to eat dinner and watch the people and hear the cacophony of voices, screams, police sirens squeals, and music blasting from the nickel jukeboxes playing the most popular, latest hits.

This beautiful porch also faced west side of Papo's house. He was a tormented soul afflicted with post-traumatic stress syndrome as a result of fighting in the Vietnam War. Across the street, our house faced the house of a family whose father and breadwinner worked the night shift.

Sitting on our porch, we heard all kinds of foul and obscene language and blessings coming out of the mouths of the little old ladies dressed in black and carrying black umbrellas as they pursued protection from the scorching rays of the island sun as well as curses and sexually-charged expletives from the young children and teenagers as they screamed at and fought each other.

We would watch the small, shoeless, and sometimes naked children screaming at the top of their lungs and running after their emaciated teenage mothers, throwing tantrums along the way while their mothers ogled their latest conquest standing at the corner store, dropping nickels inside the jukebox.

The emaciated, ashy bodies of young addicts, both male and female were a constant reminder of life in this ghetto of San Juan. Upon seeing the clear signs of a heroin overdose, the relatives, friends or just plain strangers would pick them up and hold them by their shoulders to run frantically up and down the street in an effort to bring air into their lungs and get their hearts pumping again to prevent an early death in some overgrown bushes or an unknown, hidden, murky corner.

One of those young men was not fortunate enough to have friends assist while the rush and specter of heroin took possession of his very soul, as his lids became heavy and his somnolent eyes saw the beauty of the blue sky one last time. His cloudy eyes were still open and stared blankly at the unknown, still open but not seeing the beauty of life. His face was a contortion of the mix of pain and pleasure, of a lethal rush, as white as a ghost, chalky, pasty, the last somber grimace telling a story of unknown pain. His lifeless arms still held the syringe used to inject the toxic, lethal, cloudy liquid into his young body. I saw him sitting in a crouched position by the wooden planks leading to the shanty town erected by squatter's rights by the stale, black, foul-smelling waters of the main lagoon. It was the summer of 1967.

As we sat by the porch sipping cool sodas and homemade teas, sometimes with my mom, other times by ourselves, Papo the Vietnam vet would climb atop his bed, naked as a the day he made his entrance into this world, and he would start masturbating in full view of my mom and us. We would try to divert our eyes, but to say that it was uncomfortable would be an understatement. We were downright angry and upset at being unwilling participants at his obscene show and for not being able to enjoy our porch.

My mom never complained to his parents, an elderly couple who were probably aware of their son's mental illness. She knew that it was like fighting a losing battle, but she would call us inside, close the door, and go on with her business as if nothing ever happened. Once Papo became aware that there was no audience for his freakish show when we went inside, he closed his window to maybe finish his masturbatory, five-fingered business in the loneliness of his dark room.

One night as we were sitting in the small, cramped living room sorting and bagging beauty products, we heard strange noises coming from outside in the direction of our vegetable garden. We looked at each other and in unison thought that a neighboring stray dog or cat had crawled through the fence to mess up our beautiful garden. I hurried outside just to find Vietnam Vet Peeping Tom in a stooped position, looking through the wooden slats, fully erect sausage in his hands, which moved furiously as he was enthralled by his innocent and unaware audience. The look of total surprise in his face cannot be described by mere words. As he looked at the tiny figure standing in the shadows of the night, his limp manhood shrank ten sizes too small as if he had seen a ghostly apparition, then he took off running like a madman, trampling over potted plants, metal canisters, and whatever else he found as he disappeared into the darkness. I don't think he heard the thumpitty thump, thumpitty thump of my beating heart or saw me dashing back into the house.

Remember the married man I mentioned before who apparently worked at nights? Well, he was also a freak who used to stand by the door of his house right in front of our house and touch his private parts, but he did it only when I was sitting by the porch alone while doing my homework or when I had to go past the front of his house to go to the corner store to get groceries. Many times I thought that maybe I had the word "victim" written on my forehead or maybe I had been doing something myself to be the victim or the target of so many predators, but I was OK then and I am OK now. Those men were the ones with the problem, and I just happened to be their unwilling small prey, barely twelve years old then, unable to defend myself or speak up to report the abuse.

Everyone in the community knew that my mother was a struggling single parent raising four daughters and a small boy by herself. I guess that the fear of living in such a dangerous place with four drop-dead gorgeous young daughters gnawed at her heartstrings, so she became very strict, never allowing us to have friends, associate with neighboring children, or play outside. She is and always had been a strikingly stunning attractive hard-working woman, with her waist length straight black wavy hair crowned by a patch of white hair in front, a thin waist, and the most beautiful, shapely legs I have ever seen. Both single and married men had their eyes on her, and one of them was a kind old man forty years her senior whom everyone called Mambiche.

Mambiche was retired from the merchant marine and received a pension. We never knew if he had always been single or if he was a widower, but he truly loved Mom and wanted to marry her. He would bring plates of rotisserie chicken with bread, fried plantains, and a side salad and would also bring the most delicious pastries when he came home to visit our mom. Poor Manbiche, he would cook and share his food with us, but his feelings were never reciprocated. There is one thing I know for sure, however; Mambiche was truly a gentleman who only showed great love and respect for my mom and us.

She did not respond to poor Mambiche's professions of love and acts of kindness, but she accepted the marriage proposal of a man named Narciso who was living common law with another woman a few miles from where we used to live.

Narciso gave my mom gifts such as an old stereo, a rickety black and white 19 inch television without an antenna, and a wringer top washing machine that sputtered dirty and soapy water every time it was turned on. He probably stole it from his common law wife.

A few months later, without discussing their marriage plans with her children, she married Narciso. Of course, he moved into the house with us. They slept in the little dark room that we used to live in months before, the room with the stench, nauseating odors, without windows and ventilation. Pretty soon, I realized that Narciso was a weasel of the worst kind, a poor excuse of a man who left his wife and children and thought that he was in seventh heaven when my mother accepted his proposal...a single woman with four young, beautiful daughters! The first thing he did when they married was put a lock on the refrigerator so what we had no access to the precious food he bought for himself! We managed to break the lock, of course; hungry children will always find a way.

He used to work as a janitor in a fancy hotel in Old San Juan, and every night, he brought gifts to my mom, gifts that he found in the hotel rooms or lobby. They were petty things such as scarves, earrings, bottles of wine, underwear, etc., and many times, he also bought gifts to me. If he saw me in my bedroom, usually by myself, he would put his arms around me and immediately tell me that I was tense and he could make me relax. He would try to brush my breasts with his hands, and his hands would slither down to by buttocks. I knew what he was up to and would try to leave the room; most times he would hold my hands on my back so I would not escape. One day, he brought this beautiful white and pink dress that he said that he had bought for my mom. The dress looked wrinkled and used, and it was too small for my mom! But he tried to put the dress on me by lifting my hands. Suddenly, the weasel tried to kiss my neck while my hands were up, and then he tried to fondle me. I struggled to break free and ran outside, cursing Narciso under my breath and knowing that I was not going to tell my mom; she would never believe me anyway, and she thought the world of her new beau Narciso.

One night, as we had retired to sleep in the big house, around 2:00 in the morning, I really had to relieve myself. In the process, I heard a strange noise coming from the kitchen. I got up, checked the front and back doors, went to the bathroom, and laid down in my bed again. My sister Betty preferred to sleep in a nearby cot, my two younger sisters shared a bed, and my little brother slept in his crib.

As soon as I got back from the bathroom and laid in my bed, I heard the funny, strange noise again, but disregarded it as probably a rat scurrying around the crevices as I closed my eyes trying to regain my precious sleep. All of a sudden, the noise turned into footsteps threading lightly on the creaky floor, walking very slowly and measuring every step. The scurrying rat turned out to be a dark, tall man who had come in through the window with evil intentions.

Immediately, I sat upright in the bed, petrified and holding tightly to the sheets and the pillow, as if trying to seek protection and comfort in them, trying to muffle the frenzied beating of my terrified heart. The clatters inside the house suddenly gained momentum. They were magnified a thousand times. They announced the immensity and the strength of the furious pounding of the rushing ocean waves as I shockingly tried to make some sense out of my feeble, confused thoughts. The man kept walking from the kitchen toward the living room, and suddenly, I saw his contorted dark face and his gawky silhouette trying to crouch as he came into the living room. Then he was standing by my bedroom door, looking straight at me as I sat trembling by the bed, waiting to be protected by the draped green mosquito net, the bed frame shaking as if an enormous and destructive earthquake had made its grand entrance.

My thoughts were racing and speeding as if an out of control speed train had come crashing through the house, as if a bulldozer had clamped its powerful claws and engulfed every plank, every nail, every joist, every beam, and I stood there frozen in time....

The sinewy male figure kept advancing toward me so slowly and silently that if anyone had dropped a pin on the floor it could have been heard miles away. He kept getting closer, stooping, his feral hands ready to pounce on his innocent pray, coming closer, as I remained paralyzed with fear, unable to move as I saw his face getting closer until I thought that his eyes had turned yellowish and elongated like those of a praying wild cat. He had devilish eyes and evil intentions. In the blink of an eye, a split second that seemed to last an eternity, my guttural screams that mimicked those of a wounded animal filled the sleepy house, and my tears flowed like the torrent of a thousand rivers, as the dark man dashed across the living room, his devilish slanted eyes scanning his surroundings as he tried to make a quick getaway through the front door as he became engulfed by the dark shadows of the tumultuous night.

I am pretty darn sure that he continued to hear my throaty, deep screams, my sobs as he ran away from our house. I knew the guy who tried to come into our house draped by the shadows of the night, and I cringed every time he would pass our house, nonchalant and deep in thought, as if he was planning his next attack.

The police were never called, and a report was never made since in this community, this was a daily occurrence. It was such a dangerous ghetto that the police did not come down to investigate any crimes. People shot at each other. Poor addicted souls died every day in the overgrown bushes or some street corner piled high with trash and rats as big as ferocious cats. Women fought tooth and nail over toothless, drunk, unemployed men. Macho men beat up their women right in front of everyone. Teenage pregnancy, drug use, infidelity, and child neglect and abuse were rampant, but the voices were silent. These were invisible crimes. Main Street in the big city had given life to old Boarded Up Street, to Garbage Ridden Street. It had open the avenue to give way to the corner of Vomit Street and Danger Street. I did not feel safe anymore, and then I saw it.

It appeared out of the dark, gloomy streets, raising its ugly head like a dangerous pray, its old dilapidated windows like old eyesores. People went about their daily business and did not get involved for fear of being killed. From the moment that cursed man came into our house with evil intentions, my nightmares became stronger, more frequent, more realistic, and fearsome.

The months passed, and I continued to hate nightfall. Nighttime consisted of pacing the floor, looking through the wooden slats and cracks, my desolate cries filling every room and emptying my heart. Every noise made by a scurrying rat, a screeching car, the meows of the stray cats, or the voices and laughter of every passerby were magnified a thousand times over. There I sat, in a zombielike state, wide eyes scanning every nook and cranny, fear overpowering me and robbing me of my precious sleep. The bright, emergent rays of dawn were such a welcome relief!

OH! Living in Santurce was really a trial of our survival skills, and survived I did. At school I was bullied, and I fought back like a banshee when bullied by a gang of jealous girls. I defended myself the best I could, kicked, bit, pulled hair, threw punches, and then ran as fast as I could down the street, never stopping while the flying rocks thrown by the angry girls nicked my head, shoulders, and back, stinging and hurting like hell. Soon thereafter, after many trials and tribulations, my mother announced that we were moving to the USA.

Chapter 6
Small Town-Grey Skies

Moving to the United States of America was another culture shock for me. We arrived at JFK under a terrible snowstorm, and it was so dreary, icy, and cold during that fateful day in March 1968. We had to walk a long trek through the airport tarmac, wearing short dresses and open-toed sandals. We thought that we would not make it to the main arrivals building. Our bones felt like dry sticks ready to split in twos. Our brothers had been eagerly waiting for us, carrying heavy furry coats and boots for us, which we, shivering and cold to the bone, readily embraced and welcomed like an oasis in the brutal snow and ice.

We settled in the town of Perth Amboy, New Jersey, and lived with our two older brothers, who really went out of their way to make us feel welcome. They made all the arrangements to register us in school. I passed the English reading and writing test with flying colors and was placed in a regular classroom. I had so much difficulty with understanding and speaking the language. I aced the tests but could not communicate in English. Once I went to the home economics class, and the teacher asked me to bring her some flour. I ran outside and brought her a "flower." The laughter of the children reverberates in my ears to this day. Soon after, they realized that I needed help in conversational English, so their English as a second language (ESL) program during that time involved sending me to the school's basement, a dark little room with broken students' desks and old books, musty and smelly, the smell as old as the teacher assigned to help me learn and speak English. He was an old man who slept and snored most of the time, and when he was not sleeping, he would take out his withered, dry penis and masturbate in front of me, sometimes falling asleep in the process. I would look the other way, toward the door, or close my eyes and dream of a green island with turquoise waters and balmy breezes while waiting for the school bell to ring so I could fly out of the dark cell. Like I have stated before, maybe the word victim was written all over my forehead or maybe I was such an easy prey of those men stung by the depravation, filthiness, and evil of this world. Who knows what deep, dark secrets they held?

And me? I had been in such a silent tomb for so many years, my inaudible cries never leaving my throat, the words never finding a kind ear willing to hear them, no one nearby to protect me, to hug me and tell me that everything was going to be all right, no one near, yet so many people around me. No one heard my cries or came to my aid, so I never told a soul, and the sadness within me kept growing like an ocean, its waves trying to destroy the little girl, who was swimming over and over, trying to make it to the shore.

Chapter 7

Bigger Town...Darker Skies

Due to misunderstanding and a physical fight between my sister and my brother and the fact that my mom's Adonis, Don Narciso, decided to make his getaway and left to live in Vineland, NJ with his older daughter, we moved to Passaic, NJ to a small three-bedroom apartment on Monroe Street.

It was in Passaic and at the tender age of fifteen that I found my first paying job in a factory where they manufactured bathroom and closet deodorant balls made of naphthalene. This factory was known by everyone as "The Smelly One," and at school all the students knew that I worked there due to the naphtha odor on my clothes and my coat. I made a grand $13.00 per week, however, which I always brought home to give to my mom.

During the summers, my mom would send me to live with my older brother, Junior, and his family in Perth Amboy. His wife worked at the Fedder Company, which made air conditioners. My brother worked for many years in the produce department of a local supermarket. He also loved to fish, and during the weekends he would take us to the beaches off the Jersey shores and leave us there while he went to fish. We spend the whole day at the beach, looking like burnt charcoal when he came back in the afternoon to pick us up.

Passaic...old city...old hearts...old people and a young mind. We moved to a rundown building on Monroe Street, a fifth floor walkup apartment where roaches and rats lived together, scurrying along the crevices of the creepy stairs upon hearing voices and smelling the sweat of the older men coming home tired from work. The hallways were always dark, a rotten smell permeating the old walls and encircling it as if it was trying to suffocate their tenants' existence, a smell so thick with the thousand men, women, and children who throughout the years had called it their home. We saw the landlord, Mr. Kessler, once a month, when he hurriedly walked up the decrepit stairs and banged loudly on each door, his beady eyes and dancing jowls moving rapidly with the expectation of collecting his rent money and walking down the stairs rapidly, disappearing in the mist of the sweat of the families that called the old tenement their home.

Passaic...its run-down buildings, the streets filled with garbage, the children running up and down the street happily and without a care in the world. The nearby park behind the elementary school always ready to welcome the wandering, carefree children like a mother with her arms wide open. Passaic...where the need to belong, to be accepted, the need for affection and understanding again truncated the dreams of a lonely girl and where the perverse souls once again raised their ugly heads and truncated the dreams and hopes of a lonely child.

My mother had befriended a family living on the third floor of the tenement. One member of the family was Don Juan, a younger, fortyish balding man whose previous wife had run off with another man and left him practically penniless while raising three young children, the oldest no more than five years old. Don Juan married Mrs. Alejandra, or Aleja as she was fondly called in the neighborhood, an older woman with salt and pepper wispy hair, a matronly look on her face, obese, with what seemed to be the burdens of life upon her shoulders. Mrs. Aleja had at least five grown children, I believe the youngest was about 23 years old and was living with a married man. One of her sons had just been released from jail, and she kept eyeing my older sister, Betty, as a prospective wife for her jailbird son. Another daughter had begun an affair with a younger man half her age, and she was often seen up and down Monroe Street arguing with the young girls whom she thought were after her boy toy. Oh yes! Ms. Aleja had seen much toil and trouble in her life, but she met Don Juan and apparently they hit it off. They married, and she was raising his young children. Anyone looking at Mrs. Aleja would think that she embodied kindness, trust, and acceptance and people in the community looked up to her. Mrs. Aleja, the elderly patron, the wise old woman, the generous, kindhearted soul, the savior of children. Mrs. Aleja had a dark side that no one knew, not even Don Juan, and she kept it quite a secret from her family and friends. She kept it from my mother but not from me. After a few months of our family moving to Monroe Street in Passaic, New Jersey, mom befriended Ms. Aleja. She would come often to our apartment, dragging her heavy frame of a body up the long, dark, twisty stairs, oftentimes carrying Don Juan's youngest, precious little girl. She would sit down with us and our mother to chat and drink coffee while mom took the little girl's measurements to make her dresses and hair bows. Yes, she seemed to like us and our mom. Pretty soon, her visits to our fourth floor apartment became routine, and mom was her confidante. She always commented on how well-behaved Mom's daughters were and how precious it was to have such beautiful daughters. She often mentioned her son, who needed to "settle down" and her efforts to search for a good wife for him, efforts that were fruitless because according to her, there were no real women good enough for her son out there. Her eyes often wandered, however, to where we were sitting. Many times I thought that if looks could tell the machinations of the brain, Mrs. Aleja would give away all of her secrets. She had a Machiavellian plan, and I was soon going to be led away for the kill...an innocence long gone was going to be tried and tried again. And the trust in human kindness in the form of a matronly female figure was going to be shattered again until my eyes were opened and I finally figured out the evil thoughts and plans of this lady who appeared to be mom's and our friend. She had lust and evil in her mind, old, fat and frumpy Ms. Aleja.

One Friday she came up the stairs to talk to mom, who as always was sitting in front of her old, creaky trusted sewing machine, making dresses to sell to support her family. Mrs. Aleja, chirpy as always, came in and made small talk, telling Mom how she wanted to check out the upcoming sales in the nearby town of Paterson, which at the time was thriving with booming businesses and even had a large department store called McCrory's. She told Mom how long she had wanted to go to Paterson and asked if she would allow me to go with her to the stores. I was so excited that she had selected me, the lonely, introverted, quiet, teenage girl, to be her escort to a large nearby town, a town thriving with stores, a nice soda fountain with 31 flavors of ice cream, and packed diners selling comfort foods, even a big department store! I was thrilled! I was going to nearby Paterson with mom's friend; she wanted to share her time with me! She wanted to take me to the big city! Paterson! The hustle and bustle of a large city—I could not wait to go into the stores, see the latest fashions, go into a diner, taste the food, and chat with a matronly lady, mom's trusted friend! I was so excited! And to my sheer delight, Mom said that I could accompany trusted Ms. Aleja to go to Paterson the next day.

I don't think I slept at all that Friday night. The visions of life in a big city kept moving and dancing in my head, and I felt like a princess who was getting ready for her first big dance…talk about being excited! I felt like the queen! Not the princess! I was bigger than the princess; I was the queen, selected among mom's daughters to go into this magical, large, and bustling city, ready to take on the world, to sit down and eat my really big ice cream sundae and watch people, as moms holding their little ones' hands sped by while hawking the latest sales and vendors screaming about, eyes glancing to and fro to see who was going to be their latest victim, sirens and police cars speeding down the avenue, music blasting from storefronts and a tiny, timid wide-eyed girl taking it all in, ready to see what the world had to offer.

We left about 1:00 PM on Saturday and walked along silently adown Monroe Street toward Main Street, Passaic, USA. It was a hot humid day in August. Apparently the humidity and the heat had been keeping souls indoors because I do not remember anyone walking down the street. My world was about to be shattered again, this time by a sixty-year-old matronly lady, my mom's trusted friend and confidante.

We did not speak a word while waiting for the bus that was taking us down to

114

Paterson. I was afraid of my foray into this new world, but my emotions seemed clouded by the expectations of my great shopping experience in this new world, this new city, wet, sweaty hands tightly clutching the dollar that I had been given earlier that morning...high expectations...clutching a dollar and ready to take on this new world!

We got off the rickety, old bus and walked down Main Street, never stopping to look at the stores, the sales going on, never even looking back, and not looking at the people, not even a nod of the head to acknowledge their presence. She was walking rapidly ahead and seemed to be lost in thought. I noticed that we were no longer walking down Main Street, but had veered off toward what seemed the poor section of the city, lots of boarded up buildings, closed off stores, their wooden and tin frames resembling an aged tree who is about to take its last breath, their doors no longer welcoming, but with a giant toothless grimace about to swallow a lost little girl who was now afraid at what the big city was about to become. Mom's trusted friend was beckoning me to enter the world of the lost, the world belonging to the depraved, to enter a world so dark and painful that you could hear the screams of the past victims, and then I wondered how many young little, scared, innocent little girls had entered those dark, decrepit, and revolting doors, walls that held the most innermost secrets, that held and muffled the whimpering cries of innocent victims, the doors that lead to the local hardcore pornographic movie theater.

I stood frozen in time, trying hard to tell my mind and my body to run, to run as fast as I could, but then I felt Mrs. Aleja grasp my wrist and felt the pull of her knotty, wrinkly hand on mine so strong that panic ensued. I knew that there was no way to run, no escape route; the sidewalk opened up beneath my feet, the ground was clamoring for my life, a myriad of noises and voices kept filling my head, the noises trying to muffle the voices telling me to run, and the deep voice of a trusted old lady telling me that I had to enter, that there was no other choice for me. The ground was shaking and moving, burning sweat was drenching my forehead, my arms, and my legs. Time stood still, and so did I. A strange force emanating from an elderly lady sucked me into the house of perdition.

If the smell of rancid puke and vomit was strong in the street, it was stronger and different inside the dark dungeon. It reeked of perspiration, alcohol and cheap wine, tobacco, and a thousand other revolting odors that turned my stomach into a mass of pure lard and my legs into jelly. The force kept pulling me in, however, deeper and deeper into the dark house of horrors. I felt like a lamb being led into the slaughterhouse, but the noises and words conspired with each other and refused to leave my throat. Not a sound escaped from my mouth or my lips, but the grimace, the look of pain, the disgust at what my eyes encountered once they accustomed themselves to the light is indescribable. The elderly lady looking for a glimpse of pleasure was leading me to a seat next to an elderly patron, an unshaven, dirty, stinking heap of a man whose pants were down to his knees, a dirty handkerchief covering his nakedness and his five fingers of death busily engaged in self-pleasure, his bulging eyes glancing steadily at the screen, which was showing a X pornographic film of the Argentinian porno queen Isabel Sarli. This disgrace of a human being took a glance at the whimpering little girl sitting next to him and immediately, the force of his bad breath reeking of alcohol hit me like a tornado. I remember being led to the seat next to him, and the lady sat in the next chair. I was the meat and the cheese in the middle of a sandwich…and the hand on my right side kept holding me down while a few dollars were passed between the elderly, trusted, evil lady and the disgusting heap of a man. I kept closing my eyes while all the time thinking that it was just a dream...just a dream...just a dream, but his dirty hands kept looking, kept pinching, kept touching...and then he moved and another man took his place. My nightmare was darker and somber than the place itself. I don't know if the movie lasted one hour or two or maybe three, but my nightmare and the pain of broken dreams and trust I have lasted a lifetime.

Chapter 8

Back to a Little Town...Then the Storm

While living with my brother, my job was to babysit their seven children, but I also washed and folded clothes, prepared lunch, cleaned the house and the kitchen, mopped the floors, vacuumed the rugs, etc. I did these things so that I would "earn my keep," as my brother would say, and also to earn some allowance money.

My brother and his wife, Benni, were very good friends with a family that lived across the street. They had a sixteen-year-old son named Papo who loved to come to the house to play with the children, watch television, and talk to me. All the children joked about how Papo was in love with me and that he would come only to see me. I liked Papo as a friend and did not find him attractive at all. He was shy and easygoing, and he loved to entertain the children. One day, the boys had gone to the park with the older girls, and I stayed in the house with the three youngest girls, whom I bathed, gave lunch, and put in bed for their daily nap. I then proceeded to put the washed clothes on top of the table in the formal dining room while I listened to the radio when I heard a knock at the door. Papo came in holding a can of soda and some cookies in his hands. He proceeded to sit in the dining room making small conversation while I continued dividing and folding clothes. He asked about my brother and my sister-in-law, the older children, and the youngest one. All of a sudden, making sure that we were all by ourselves in the downstairs room, he got up, came behind me, and overpowered me with all his strength, telling me how he had been in love with me all along, how he wanted to kiss me, and how much he wished I would pay attention to him. I was telling him to please leave because my brother was supposed to be coming. He became enraged. As I struggled to become free of his embrace and his advances, he became angrier and

121

enraged, biting me on my ears and my neck to the point of hurting me while at the same time, grabbing my face and twisting it to face him so that he could kiss me. He kept telling me that it was all my fault because I had refused to be his girl and that he was going to get what belonged to him anyway. He then threw me on the floor. I landed on my stomach while he forced himself on me from the back. He raped me right then and there. When he heard the footsteps of my niece coming down the stairs, he immediately got up, zipped his pants, and left rapidly through the front door, his unbutton plaid shirt exposing his dark flesh and his khaki pants stained with the wet semen that he had just left inside my unwilling body. Afterwards, my brother and his wife would ask me and the children about Papo. He would stop by and sheepishly ask for forgiveness, but I did not want to speak to him nor listen to his excuses and avoided all eye contact. I guess that I was still in shock for what he had done to me, a person who professed to love me and who was always so respectful toward the family. His visits became less frequent until he stopped coming all along. The last I heard of him was that his family had moved to Connecticut, and I never saw him again.

Chapter 9

Big City-Bright lights-Broken Dreams

Again, it was while visiting my brother in Perth Amboy that I met the one destined to be the father of my first child. I saw Red when he drove his stepmother, Elba, to visit my sister-in-law Benni. I was seventeen and fell in love with his brownish khaki uniform from the Marine Corps, his joking personality, and his curly, bright red hair. He was all talk and no action, a roving eye, a ladies man who had a girlfriend in every corner and despised work like water despises fire. But I thought that I was in love and never saw the writing on the wall. After about three months of courtship, I eloped with him and went to live with his mother, Maria, in Brooklyn, New York. She was a tenderhearted, larger than life kind of woman who took me under her wings, embraced me, and showed a different kind of love. She treated me like the daughter she never had but always admonished me for eloping with her son, whom she loved dearly but knew that he was not cut out to be a husband. We would get up very early every day to search for jobs, and fortunately I found a job in a light bulb factory during the second shift. She showed me how to get on and off the subway train and would prepare lunch for me. She would make sure that her son was waiting for me when I got off work to escort me home. One day that she told me to stay home and sent her son to look for a job, reprimanded him for being lazy, and told him that he needed to find a place for him and his wife to live because he had decided to get married.

We then went to live with his aunt until we both found work, but he never got up early and stated that he could not find any work. His heart was into music, and he had his own band. They were very good and found gigs all over the place, but his earnings went into drugs. I would wait for hours on end, looking at the window and waiting on Red to come home.

Sometimes, the hours because days and the days became weeks. It was like he had been swallowed by the depths of the earth, only to reappear stoned, sleep for days, and eat like a horse. The vicious cycle would then start all over again. Upon finding out that I was pregnant with my firstborn, I finally moved back with Maria. With "off the book" earnings and my measly welfare check, once I had my baby son, Angel, I was able to secure a two-bedroom apartment in the same building, on the fifth floor, apartment seventeen. I managed to furnish and decorate my little apartment. Finally, Red left me for another woman who was having his baby.

I stayed alone with a newborn son, new apartment, and a broken heart! How I cried for days on end, cried on Marias's shoulder, cried myself to sleep when I thought that all hope was gone. He told me that he could not live with me because I was a wimp, an ineffective coward unable to support him in his quest to be a great musician, and for many years I thought of myself of being a coward, unable to face life itself, unable to come to terms with my broken up, sad, lonely life, but I had something more going on for me that time. I had this tiny person who depended on me for his every need; my son needed me this time around.

I remember the building's owner, Mr. Pymm, coming around to collect his rent and telling me that he could lower my rent if I was "nice" to him. I was never nice to him and always paid my rent promptly and in full because throughout my life, men had never been nice to me, and I knew that he was not the exception. It was also while living in this apartment that I decided that I was not going to live the rest of my life having children and living on a government subsidy. I decided to go to school during the nights that I did not work in order to earn my GED. I passed my GED with flying colors.

It was while living at this apartment by myself that I met skinny Iris and her four children, ages thirteen through five, and one of them would become the love of my life, my true and only friend in life, my lover, and the one who has been with me during sickness and love, for richer or poorer, and will be with me until death us do part. The teenagers and children in the building loved to come to my apartment just to hang out and Iris' children were no exception. They would come and watch television until the wee hours of the night, play cards, or just talk. I was a teenager just like them, but I had a child and my own apartment. Iris worked at night just like any other single lady in the neighborhood just to make ends meet and would give me some money to babysit her children. Other times she would just leave them alone in her apartment, and I would keep an eye on them. They were sooo bad! They smoked cigarettes and weed, drank beer, were streetwise and would use more profanity than a sailor, but they were also very loving and wise and cringed when they saw their mom with a belt in her hands, scrambling like elves looking for the nearest place to hide. They would run up and down the fire escape and play on the roof overlooking the Williamsburg Bridge. They knew all the shortcuts and people in the community and also fought like Marines on a battlefield. Her oldest son became a true Marine, and he is the love of my life. I was eighteen years old then and was not aware that true love had knocked at my door.

It would take many years until I saw my true love again. I moved away, and he went into the Armed Forces. We would not see each other for years.

Chapter 10

Haunting Small Towns

After getting my GED I then completed a Work Incentive Program offered by the Agency for Income Maintenance, or public assistance for single females. I registered, and while studying typing and office procedures, I would leave my son in Passaic with my mom and sisters, traveling back and forth during weekends to stay with my son and studying. Once I completed the course and passed my typing test, I was able to find a job in a typing pool with the Internal Revenue Service in downtown New York City; I was so proud of myself!

It was during one of my public transportation trips to Passaic that I met Ricco, the father of my daughter, Candy. He was younger than me, tall, dark, debonair, and he had the gift of gab, a spoiled only son who thought that the sun came out only for him and seemed so surprised upon learning that I was an older woman of 21 years old, had my own apartment in New York, was employed by a federal agency, and had fallen prey to his advances. He was so suave and convincing, and I was unaware that he also had lived a turbulent, abused life at the hands of a step-father.

I moved back to Passaic with my new found boyfriend, gave up my apartment, and lived one of the darkest, most painful period in my life. Unknowingly, my life would take an unexpected turn. I would live in torment, a dark tornado where I experienced horrendous moments of excruciating physical, sexual, and emotional violence, a violence so humiliating that not even an animal should be subjected to such treatment, no less a human being, not even a vulnerable female. No one but I survived.

I was still working in New York and commuting during the week and soon after, had to leave my job due to pregnancy. Since Ricco was not working and was unable to provide for the family, I had to apply for public assistance and food stamps. While working and, therefore, coming home late, I would stop by my mother's house to pick up my son and then walk about two miles to get home. Most of the time, he would wait for me by the stairs. Once at the house, he grabbed me by the hair and pulled with all his might, screaming at me for being late and for dinner not being done. Other forms of abuse included taking away every bit of my money left after the bills were paid, not allowing any contact with my family, name calling, and cursing at my son. Once, he even cut off the outside phone line so that I would not be able to make telephone calls. Every day the abuse escalated and got worse. I had to put up with obscene words, punching, pinching, and hair-pulling, and I stopped working altogether due to my pregnancy.

I was home all day long, cleaning, washing his clothes by hand, cooking, and trying to obey his childish commands, but the abuse never stopped. He would punch my face and my stomach without mercy. He would punch my back with all his might. He would hit me in my eyes and mouth, while at the same time screaming obscenities at the top of his lungs, while my son and I cowered in a corner, trying not to cry out loud so that his mother would not hear us. At one time, he grabbed his penis and a knife and dared me to cut it. I was whimpering and so afraid to even grab the knife, then he took the knife and put it to my throat, his eyes flaming with hate, and white spittle foaming at the ends of his mouth. His face contorted into a smirk so evil that every hair on my body stood on end. Again, no one heard my cries. Most times, it gave him pleasure to drag me by my legs, while throwing my son into the other room and locking the door, my son's cries filling the house and my soul.

Afterwards, he would drag me to the bedroom to "make love to me" as he would say. A bloody mass of my suffering body just laid there, withholding every cry while he satisfied his manly desires, excruciating punches still flying around and landing on the agonizing twisted form of my body, punches coming and going. The beatings continued and then the brutal thrusting, the savage biting and the gushing of bodily fluids, staining the sheets with a weak mix of blood, bodily fluids, urine, and tears. Those acts were so savage, so painful, and so degrading to me that my only instinct was to survive the nightmare and put an end to either his life or my life. I always wondered about the baby inside me, how she was going to survive abuse so inhumane, the shock and blows to my body. But soon afterwards, my baby girl was born, beautiful, healthy, and radiant. Thinking back then, my thoughts revolved only around my children, their safety and well-being. It was never about me since spiritually and emotionally, I was dead already. As soon as he left the house, I started exploring and weaving in my mind a successful method to kill him so that the nightmare would end.

Many times I wondered about the reasons for such treatment against a person, a human being, but then again, I reasoned that it was never about me. One day my sister came unexpectedly to the house. She observed my black eyes, busted lips, swollen face, and my grimace from the pain of broken ribs upon trying to hug her. She saw the slow, lingering tears and took me and my children to the police department, only to take a report and give me a date to come back.

Where was I going to live? Where would I go? If I went to my family, would they bring more pain and abuse to the ones close to me? It had been my fault all along. I could not share any more pain with my loved ones, could not let them witness my foreseeable demise, so like the good, submissive woman that I was, I went back to my house. There I was subjected to another beating and more threats if I even thought of attending the hearing, which I did and sheepishly told the judge that I had fallen down the stairs and hit my head in the process. I must have looked so funny or maybe entertaining with my black patch covering my left eye like a swashbuckling pirate and my black swollen trembling lips because the judge smirked and faster than the blink of my covered eye, dismissed my case and went on to the next order of business for the day. My fate had been sealed.

This was the turning point in my life, when I decided that becoming a killer was not the answer. Again, and I kept thinking about my small children, so I listened to that small, inside voice telling me run for my life, to run with my children, to leave all possessions behind and seek a safe haven, regain my sanity, and become a woman again. All along during that dark period, I had felt like trash, his favorite term of endearment, and worse than hearing those words over and over was actually believing them.

I waited silently until his shadow disappeared around the corner and gathered the most important documents that I knew would be needed once I made my getaway, birth certificates, social security cards, immunization cards, and the last $50.00 left over after paying the rent. I dressed my children with a double set of clothes, put diapers and three bottles of milk in an old bag, and ran for my life, ran as fast as I could, the wind behind my back, heart pounding strong as if wanting to jump out of its cavity and get ahead of me. I kept glancing back as my eyes scanned the street behind me, ahead of me, making sure that no one was hiding behind bushes ready to pounce and drag me back to hell and that the sinewy shadow was no longer chasing me. I was running, running, running for safety, running for my life, while I held tightly to my son's hand, and the house off Summer   Avenue   was getting smaller, smaller until it was no more. At one point it seemed like a little dark dot in the map of my life, a dot that I was sure I would never encounter again. I had broken free of my captivity, I had been stepped upon, broken down, and humiliated, but I fought back. I survived, and I had delighted in the sweet taste of freedom.

It seemed as if it took forever to get to downtown Main Street, where I crouched down, tired, exhausted but free, towing two of my most precious possessions, glancing up and down, east and west to make sure that I had not been followed while I waited for the bus heading down the Lincoln Tunnel, to New York, to my newfound freedom and my new life…but I was not aware that I would be faced with yet another challenge.

Chapter 11

Big City...Dark lights...Trail of Tears

It seemed as if I had waited for hours for the bus that would take me to my new found freedom. When it finally came, I boarded the bus with my prized possessions at hand, my children, my documents, and a few dollars. I sat in the back of the bus, pensive about a brighter future. Arriving in the city, I felt overwhelmed by the fumes emanating from the Lincoln Tunnel, noise, and the millions of car and taxis weaving in and out of traffic until we reached our destination, Grand Central Station. The throngs of people hurrying about, the vendors calling out their wares, the smells of the city, and the deafening noise of the underground subways were a bit terrifying, and I stopped to think about my next move. I boarded the next train that arrived, not knowing its destination. I just needed a place to rest, relax, and get my thoughts together. I rode the train for about two days, the children sleeping in my lap, leaving the train station only to use the public bathrooms, wash my children's other change of clothes and get water to prepare powder milk, which I had packed in a little plastic baggie.

I went to a public phone to inform my loved ones about my quick getaway and to let them know I was safe and in New York. I did not tell them about my whereabouts and that I had no other place to go. I did not want to worry them with my problems, something that I had brought upon myself. As long as they knew that I was safe, it was OK. They asked me to go back to live with them, but I adamantly refused, knowing that the devil in sneakers was lurking around, mad as a rabid animal and that he would hurt my family and anyone willing to help me. I refused their offers to help, and they informed me that he had been to their houses looking for me and he had threatened my mother, even pulling out a gun. My mother and sisters called the police, but by the time they arrived, he was long gone. I also called my older son's grandmother, an angel named Maria, who also informed me that he had been to her house but that she had put him in his place. She was a no nonsense type of woman, strong and determined to protect her grandson at all costs. She told me to hide in her son's, Louie's, apartment in a public housing project in the city. She gave me the address. Thanking her, I headed to Delancey Street in lower Manhattan to a safe haven, or so I thought.

It just happened that Maria, in her desire to help, did not tell Louie or his common law wife, Margie, that I was coming. I knocked on the door only to see a strange face looking at me and asking me what was my purpose for knocking at the door. Margie seemed angry, and she had every right to be because no one informed her about my situation. Louie had moved in with her recently upon finding out that she was expecting his baby. He was unemployed and living off the dole, the measly food stamps that Margie received, and here was this strange woman, knocking at her door, asking for refuge. Soon after, Louie also came to the door and asked me to come in. I explained my situation, but Margie was not receptive at all. I asked permission to shower and bathe my children, and she said that it was ok. She asked me politely, however, not to use the stove or anything in the kitchen, since they had just finished dinner and the kitchen had been cleaned. One of her rules was that once the kitchen was cleaned, no one was allowed to use it. I just fed my children powdered milk, Vienna sausages, and crackers and proceeded to sleep in the floor with my children. I felt so humiliated and alone that night, but at least my children had clean sheets and a corner to sleep in.

The next morning I lied to them and told them that my guardian angel, Maria, had told me that the coast was clear and that I was going to Brooklyn to stay with Maria. I left early that day, never to see Margie again. Again, I used the subways days and nights as my humble abode, never leaving the station so that I would not pay the fare again. One of the biggest problem I faced was that I could not go to the local public assistance in New York because when I was in Passaic, I had received food stamps and my monthly check. I had to wait for a whole month, or so the lady at the window at the local Income Maintenance Center on Montague St. had told me. I was up the creek without a paddle, terrified to tell anyone about my situation, homeless, living in subways and parks, resting and sleeping on park benches, scared out of my wits thinking that something could happen to me and my children. At that point I could not figure out what had been worse, living in a hopeless domestic violence situation or being homeless not knowing where the next piece of bread was coming from, not having a bed to sleep in or a warm shower. I decided to go to the public assistance office one more time. If there were shelters for homeless women and children or victims of domestic violence, then no one told me. I was not going to tell the lady behind the window for fear that she would take my children away. I had to make one last effort before going through with Plan B.

In my desperate state of mind during that time, Plan B seemed like the safest, most appropriate thing to do. I said to myself that I was going to try to get some help one last time, and if it did not work out, I was not going to drag my children through the mud and uncertainty of my life anymore. They deserved better. They deserved the best things in life, and if I could not afford to give them a future, then I would take us out of our misery and end our lives once and for all. I had reached the end of my rope. I was tired of running, tired of crying. I was hurting inside, every bone, every muscle wanted to rest, every drop of blood and sweat within me had lost its will to live. I was giving up.

That night, while sitting on a park bench, I wrote my goodbye note to whoever would find our lifeless, mangled bodies with a short explanation for my drastic decision. After a long night and a river of tears and everlasting hugs, I had decided that I was going to jump in front of ten thousand pounds of steel coming at me at sixty miles an hour. I was going to jump in front of the train while holding tightly to my children's small, innocent hands. Another angel would soon spread her wings.

I had decided to go to the public assistance office one last time, with the hope of getting help. If not, then Plan B would be in full effect. That day, however, my angel was right behind me in the waiting lane. Apparently, she had seen something in me. If not the tears, then it must have been my demeanor, my sadness, my desperation, or my children's dirty, sticky faces or their unkempt clothes. She was wearing a mid-length printed floral dress, black sandals that apparently had seen many sidewalks. Her brown, soft, and silky hair reached all the way to her waist. She had beautiful skin that seemed to glow in the sun. Her hands were refined and smooth, and her fingers were as delicate as petals. She was so calm and relaxed. She was not an apparition. Her name was Helen. She was only eighteen years old, and she was also at the office to apply for food stamps.

Her name is derived from the Greek language, and it means "sun ray, shining light". When the Catholic bishop made a special visit to my hometown in 1958, many children attended church that day to attend a mass confirmation by the archbishop. I was one of those children, and he pronounced my name in Latin but to be known in English as Raymonda, which means "light of the world". Regarding this etymology of our names, I honestly believe that our names were scrambled and transposed. Helen became my guardian and protector when she saw that Raymonda's light within her soul was about to dim and become extinct. Was it a coincidence? I don't think so.

In my life, there have never been coincidences, happenstances or chances, as I believe that everything happens for a reason. We were both at the same place, at the right time, and somehow, she knew my heartache. She knew that I needed help, that I was dying inside and that I had no one to turn to, or so I thought. There is a saying that people come into your life for a reason, a season, or a lifetime, and Helen came into my life for a specific reason. Every day of my life since then, I have silently thanked Helen for having a heart of gold as big as the world, for her random act of kindness, and for coming into my life that fateful, hazy summer day in July 1977.

Although she was only eighteen years old, she was also married and had one baby boy the same age as my daughter. She followed me down to the nearby park and told me that he overheard the conversation between the case worker and me, and

148

she wanted to help me. She said that she did not have much, a little one-bedroom apartment in the Bushwick section of Brooklyn, off Myrtle Avenue close to the elevated train. The building was so old that it shook like an earthquake every time the M train passed nearby. Her husband was also very young and worked in a factory, not making enough to support his family. They had a small walk-up apartment in the fourth floor that consisted of a bedroom, a bathroom, and a small kitchen. Right next to the bathroom she had found enough room to put her son's small crib, and most of the family's belongings were in cardboard boxes for lack of dressers. She covered the boxes with colorful sheets and put pictures and mementos on top of the boxes to give her little apartment that lived-in feeling.

There was hardly any space in the cramped living room, enough for a small sofa and an old black and white television. Her apartment was small, cramped, and dark, but when I entered with all my belongings in a scrappy bag and my two precious possessions, I had entered the most beautiful, elegant Vanderbilt Castle!

She immediately cooked for us; whatever she cooked it was delicious wand we were ravenous. We had not eaten a good meal in weeks! She made me feel so welcome, unlike Margie, and told me that I could stay for as long as I wanted. She folded some baby blankets and divided her son's crib into two, one side for her son and one side for my daughter. She looked for blankets and pillows in order for me and my son to sleep on her sofa, and she also told me to feel free to use anything in her house. Helen later informed me that she had grown up in a Christian house and she saw something different, something special in me when standing behind me at the public assistance office. Her heart had been filled with love, and she knew that she needed to protect me. When she had errands to do, I would stay in her apartment, cleaning, tidying it up, cooking, and washing the babies' clothes or whatever else needed to be done. If she had to cook in the evening, I would take the rolling grocery cart full of sheets, clothes, etc., and carry it on my back down four flights of stairs to go across the street to the Laundromat. I always wanted to do something to let her know how appreciative I was and how much I valued her kindness. Helen was so special, so loving, and so kind. She was an angel sent my way in my desperate hours. I could have kicked myself over and over for not thinking straight during that time. I knew her name was Helen, but in my broken, painful and messy reality, I never asked her for a last name, never asked for her husband's or her baby's names. Never asked for additional information just in case I needed to thank her one day…Just Helen, as beautiful as a virgin and as lovely both inside and outside as a fresh, summer flower.

I had been on the run exactly one month, the last two weeks with Helen and her family, and I knew that my time to move on had come. I knew that they had approved my public assistance benefits, and I gave half of my food stamps to Helen, which she politely declined. We hugged and cried together and she wished me the best. I thanked her for her love and help and told her that I would be back to see her soon. She knew that I had called some relatives and that my daughter's father had resigned himself to the fact that I was long gone and he was no longer looking for me. My sister wired me some money to tide me over, for subway tokens and clothes for my children, and I ended up in Maria's house, in Williamsburg. It was the same building where I had lived years ago, where I obtained my first apartment, my GED diploma through the nightly efforts of a no-nonsense teacher Ms. Carrero, my typing classes, my first job with the IRS, the place where years before I had met my one and only love face-to-face and let him go for a while.

When Maria saw me for the first time that day her sobs were like piercing knives in my heart; again, I had made a loved one cry. She had been so worried for me and her grandchildren and could not believe the lifeless skeleton weighing eighty pounds and the sunken, terrified, baggy eyes. Where once stood a long, curly, silky head of hair now stood frizzy white hairs with missing clumps and bald patches, a shadow of my former self standing in front on her. My beautiful teenage smile was no longer there, replaced by a crooked grimace. Sadness came across whenever I attempted a smile. Like a flash flood, tears came down and would not stop, as if attempting to wash my pain away. She hugged me for what it seemed like an eternity, and we both cried for such a long time. How I loved Maria and how much I miss her touch! How much I admired her wisdom, her outlook on life, her smile when the world around her seemed to fall apart, and her passion for everything in life. Helen came into my life for a reason and stayed such a short time, but Maria came into my life for a season and stayed in my heart forever!

Again, I came back to Maria's house, carrying my meager belongings in the old bag that had shared bits and pieces of my life. Once we said our hellos, I sat down on her brown sofa, and she told me, "You are pregnant." I could not believe it. I could not afford another child. I could not physically nor mentally carry another baby. I had nothing left within me. I felt as if ten thousand gallons of ice cold water had been dumped on top of me. I was numb, shocked, angry, and I knew that I was still homeless with two young children. I could not bring another child into this world to be homeless, hungry, and hopeless.

The Dream

He was such a cute, chubby little precious baby boy. He was supposed to be a newborn, but he looked as if he was six months old. He was swaddled in in baby blue blankets with cartoon animal prints that seemed to tickle him whenever he was touched. His eyes were enormous, round, and brown and were framed by the longest black, thick lashes I had ever seen. He had a full head of black, shiny, silky hair; when I ran my hand through that wonderful hair, it felt like strands of silk while getting tangled in my fingers. His skin was so soft and healthy, warm to the touch, and he had a peaches and cream complexion. He responded to my soft caress with a wiggle of his tiny hands and feet, and I swear that a saw a glimpse of a twinkle of his eyes and a mischievous smile on his chubby little face. He was just gorgeous, and he felt so comfortable in my arms.

I carried him everywhere, and I kept thinking, "My baby, my sweet baby, I will never let you go." I heard my hubby saying, "Put him down or you will spoil him rotten!" I remember my response very well, "This is my baby, and I will take care of him and carry him for the next thirty years!"

All of a sudden, I heard the ding, ding, ding of my dog's collar and woke only to find my arms empty again and my eyes flowing with burning tears as I realized that I just had the most beautiful, sad, recurring dream of a mother who longs for her child that will never be there.

My beautiful child whose life was cut short by the most heart-wrenching, difficult decision a woman can ever make, whose lungs never filled with the precious, life-giving gulps of air, who was never caressed by loving hands, never held tight. His memory will live forever in my heart, and my arms will forever long to hold him, embrace him, caress him, and never let him go...the dream...oh! How I wish to see my baby again only if in a dream!

It was a very difficult, heart-wrenching decision for me, but at the time, it seemed like the most appropriate one. I was between a rock and a hard place, with no job, no place to live, no furniture, and no hope. Life had been sucked out of me. I had no one to counsel me, no Planned Parenthood, no social services, nor counseling for abused women and children, no future, nothing. I did not tell Maria about my decision, but I went to a women's clinic off Broadway near the South Side. They completed the pregnancy testing, which, of course, was positive. I made arrangements to come again within a few days to terminate the pregnancy in order to go on with my life. I still dream about that day and what my life could have been if I had been able to keep my baby. The dream is always the same...a mother caressing the most beautiful baby boy in her arms, but then I wake up only to realize that it is just a dream. This dream always brings such hurting, aching pain inside because I know that the dream will never become a reality.

A week later I went to visit Helen to let her know that I was OK and to, again, thank her for her kindness. She was not at home. I returned a few days later at a different time, and she was not at home. I returned again for a third time, and as I was walking toward her apartment, I saw the bright orange sign, "Room for Rent". I ran up the stairs, choking and holding on to the banisters as if they were lifesavers and knocked on the door, but only the silence responded. When I heard the creeeakkk of a door opening next door and a little old lady peeking at me, telling me that the young family had moved and asking if I wanted to rent the apartment, I knew that my guardian angel had been given another mission and was off somewhere helping another poor soul. I sat by the stairs, silently calling out her name, but I knew that her treasure was waiting for her.

I stayed with Maria for about three months, always cleaning, cooking, washing, ironing, etc., to at least reimburse her for her kindness. Sometimes in the evenings or hot summer nights, I would sit on the stoop of the building of Metropolitan Avenue, immersed in my thoughts and pondering about my life. Cars came and went, people exited the subways, going home to their families, children played in the nearby park, everyone looked so happy, but I kept looking at the street and the cars going by toward New York City, toward Queens and Long Island, looking far and trying to reminisce about happier times in my life, which were very few.

Right next door there was an Italian bakery, and its owner's name was Tina. She was an Italian immigrant widow who had settled in Greenpoint, and her husband and brother, Phil, had opened up a bakery years before. The aroma of freshly baked bread and almond-filled cookies permeated the street and

159

were indeed delicious! In the evening, commuters would stop at the bakery to bring home brown bags of the delicacies baked by Miss Tina. She was usually by herself at the bakery and before closing time, would call me into the bakery, wrap up some day-old bread and cookies and would say, "Take this to your kids." Such a kind woman. If she was by herself at the bakery during the day, I would go into the store, not looking forward to day-old bread, but just to keep her company and help without expecting any payment in return. She would send me to the store to get her groceries and to the deli across the street to get her a sandwich or something to drink. She would eat half of her sandwich and would share the other half with me.

Some days before closing time, I would clean the bathroom, sweep and mop the floor, take out the trash to the green dirty dumpster located at the back of the alley, or just made sure she was OK. You see, Ms. Tina used to walk with a cane, and it was hard for her to get around. We helped each other out, and sometimes, Ms. Tina would slip a twenty dollar bill inside the pocket of my pants and would give me a loaf of bread and tell me in Italian, "Take this to Maria." I guess angels come in all sizes, colors, ages, and shapes and speak different languages.

One day, I was in the bakery and asked Tina if one of her friends had an apartment or a room for rent for a single mother and two children. I explained to her that ever since I moved in with Maria, I had been knocking on doors, checking the want ads for apartments, kept asking around without luck. It was not that I did not longer wanted to live with Maria, but she had a small two-bedroom apartment, and her son Louie was living with her, leaving me his small bedroom while he had to sleep in a couch in the living room. With a big smile on her face, Tina told me that her beloved husband had bought a multiple apartment building in Bushwick many years ago and that she had a vacancy!

I arranged to go see the apartment off Wilson Avenue a few days later and met with her daughter. I immediately fell in love with the railroad style apartment, and Tina accepted half of a month's rent and did not ask me for a security deposit. I had an apartment!!!

I moved in the same week, although I had nothing to move. I changed my address and registered my son at school. Someone gave me a set of twin beds, which were missing a leg, and I put them side by side with a piece of wood to balance out one of the beds. The sheets were given to me by a nun at the local St. Anthony of Padua Thrift Shop, and my bed was an old blue sofa that my son and I dragged from the curb about two blocks away. For pots and pans I went again to the thrift shop with a letter from the public assistance agency, and they helped out. We would sit on the old blue sofa to have dinner, and they were some of the most delicious meals ever. We were together, had a place to live, had a place to sleep, and it came with great sacrifices, but it was our place. We would walk three miles to go see Maria at least every Saturday or weekend, and she would help with a towels, clothes, etc. Her son never helped with anything, but she knew that I had a need for whatever came my way. We would also stop by to see Tina, and sometimes she saved an old table, a figurine, or some knickknacks that she would carefully put in a shopping bag along with some cookies and bread. We were a family again, we were together, and I thank God every day that I was not strong enough to bring Plan B into full effect.

In October 1978, my son was in first grade, and I applied for daycare for my daughter, telling my caseworker that I had gotten a job at a local clothes store in nearby Knickerbocker. I lasted one day! I was not cut out to be a saleslady, and in the afternoon I informed my supervisor that I had been accepted into a community college and I needed to have some time off so that I could go to the admissions department to start the process. I asked for a shift change to the evening or closing hours. I had no idea who was going to watch my children in the evening after coming home from college and then going to work, but I was determined that I was going to college. I had taken the acceptance letter from Hostos Community College to my caseworker, and she was tickled that she had a client that was going to college.

I had told myself that I was not going to stay living off the public dole for the rest of my life, having little ones running around barefooted and hungry. I knew that I could handle the coming challenges. The worst was behind me. I had daycare and schooling for my oldest son, and the future was ahead of me. The supervisor at the clothing store told me not to come back to the store the next day, and you know what? I was happy that for the first time that I had been terminated from my job, on the first day no less!

Choa lived on the second floor and had three small little ones of her own, and we watched each other's kids every so often. She was also the auntie of the love of my life whom I had met four years earlier when I lived on the fifth floor on Metropolitan Avenue. She also informed me that Pops as he was lovingly called by his family, the love of my life, my friend, my confidant had gone on to the Marines and was somewhere in Japan. Or was it the Philippines or Okinawa? I don't know, but he had gone on to see the world. He was no longer a skinny, brawling little kid from the south side of Brooklyn. He had been halfway around the world, had seen other lands, had become a proud Marine, a true man in every sense of the word, and he found me living on Wilson Avenue with two children when he came to see me one winter evening in December such a long time ago.

He carried a bunch of beautiful, bright red roses in one hand and a bottle of

165

wine in the other, and nervously knocked on my door, not knowing how I was going to take his visit. He was dressed in his sharp, neatly pressed Marine Corp uniform and was so handsome! We hugged each other for what seemed like an eternity, as I felt a tear drop slowly caressing my cheek...being oh so careful not to mess up his khaki crisp uniform! My children loved him, and he also brought gifts for them. We talked forever, and that night, on the raggedy, torn blue sofa from the curb department store, we became intimate for the first time.

My Pops! We had been through so much together. We have known each other for the last 45 years. I still remember when he told me that he loved me and wanted to live with me. He was only an innocent thirteen year old child, such a young gentleman, so sweet and proper. At that time I was seventeen and I remember telling him to come back when he became an adult. Since his visit that day on Wilson Avenue, we   have   been together for the last thirty-five years. We have been together through thick and thin, through tears and laughter, in richness and poverty, and our love has grown more with each passing day. We have smoked weed together and snorted coke together, worked together and cried together. We have been separated due to military deployments and have missed each other terribly. He supported me through college, and I told him that he could also do the same thing. That was his incentive to register in college, and once we moved to Georgia, he completed his degree.

He worked odd jobs once he left the Marine Corps. He worked in a clothing store, as a driving school instructor, and as a driver making deliveries to different companies around JFK Airport. I would accompany him on my days off from college. I remember that one day he forgot his company gas card; we had no money and needed gas. We stopped at this gas station in Rockaway, and he offered to get gas and then come back to pay. The attendant did not want any of that, however. He asked him to leave his beautiful girlfriend behind and then come back for her, as a goodwill gesture that he was going to return. He said, "no way, Jose," and drove off. We laughed so hard that when I asked him if he would leave me behind, he said that he would always be close to me. We were always together, we were soul mates, skin and nails, and we are still are.

Once he realized that he was not going anywhere in those dead end jobs, he applied to the Army Reserves and was accepted back in the Armed Forces. He was able to retire from that program after twenty-seven years!

One Christmas I cried so much over not being able to buy toys and clothes for my kids because we were not making enough, and it was the year of the Cabbage Patch Craze. My daughter wanted one of those dolls so bad that I used to cry myself to sleep at night thinking that I was not going to be able to purchase her doll. It broke my heart and kept me thinking that my struggles were too much, that I was not doing everything I could. I remember telling her to write a letter to Santa, that maybe her dream of having a Cabbage Patch doll would come true, but I was so afraid after I told this to my sweet little girl.

I could not take my words back and prayed for a miracle on our way to the local post office to mail her carefully handwritten note to Santa. Three days before Christmas, my heart leapt for joy when a small package arrived in the mail addressed to my daughter. This note is for whoever performed a good deed that helped my daughter get her doll. If one day you read this, if you remember going to the local post office and picking up a note written by an anxious little girl, let me tell you that you performed a miracle, you changed the life of a little girl and the heart of a struggling mother. You will be blessed for the rest of your life.

Your kindness will be returned to you a thousand fold, and your children will be blessed because your act of random kindness brought tears of joy to a little girl in Brooklyn, New York.

All this time, I was going to City College after graduating from Hostos Community College and proud to admit that I did not pay one penny for my education, thanks to this great country. My caseworker never bothered me during the recertification process which was required every six months in order to continue getting welfare benefits. When I showed her my transcripts and grades, she would beam with pride and give me thumbs up. There were months when she would just mail me the recertification form with a request to mail her a copy of my college registration or grades. Through my City College years, I was an A student and always on the Dean's List or Honor Roll. If I had to walk miles to get to City College, I would. My education was that important to me. I wrote and typed papers for other students, did research, sold arts and crafts, wrote speeches, anything to make a dollar to save and help me buy subway and bus tokens, lunch, and books for school. I was that determined to finish what I had started.

I was selected for the Tuition Assistance Program, Pell grants, SEEK Program in New York State, which stands for Seeking Education and Excellence through Knowledge. I also did some work study in order to be gainfully employed while attending college. I was selected to be a lifetime member of Psy Beta and the Golden Key Honor Society which are national honor societies for exceptional students excelling in academics. I proudly became a member of Who's Who in Minorities in the USA. I received a letter of recommendation from New York Senator Representative Mario Biaggi, and I was very proud of my accomplishments. I worked for the Dean of the Psychology   Department and the Bursar's Office. The proudest moment in my life, other than attending my graduation, was when I was able to take my Bachelor of Arts degree in Psychology to my elderly case worker at the Public Assistance Office and ask her to close my case while giving her a hug and a big smile. I could tell that it was also one of her proudest moments too. She was truly one of a kind, and she believed in me.

I knew that I had landed a state job right after graduation because the need for case managers to investigate incidents of child abuse and neglect was so great, and the outlook was dismal.

It was also during this time that I found out that one of the people who truly helped me in life had met a tragic, unexpected death; I was devastated upon learning that Ms. Tina had died. She had always treated me with decency and like the daughter she never had, and her kindred spirit did not deserve such a horrific death. I learned that when trying to cross the busy street while struggling with her cane, she had been run over by a delivery truck, and her broken body lay in the middle of the big avenue, her intestines spilling out and every one of her bones broken from the impact. It was a closed casket wake and a beautiful funeral; she deserved to be happy in death.

A week after getting my degree in psychology from the City College of New York, I had landed a job as a case manager with the Department of Social Services, black little notebook and all. Mrs. M was our training supervisor, and about ten of the newbies had the easiest cases to "investigate".

I was a child protective services investigator, and my responsibilities were to ensure that children were not abused or maltreated. I was there to save every child in Kings County, New York. What an irony, the poster child of childhood and teenage abuse trying to protect children from further abuse, and the mistakes that I made! Goodness! As I look back I think of so many children that needed to be taken out of their homes. During my tenure as a child protective worker, I saw and heard things that not even adult eyes are not supposed to see. I had no driver's license, so I took the elevated train, the bus, or the subway everywhere. If there was a need to remove a child from the parent's home, I was always alone, and my instructions were to call the Big Apple taxi with the approval of the in line supervisor or whoever was in charge that day.

There was no protection, no visiting by two caseworkers, no mace, pepper spray, or stun guns to protect against the irate parents and family members when removing the little ones or even just asking questions. Sometimes if there was a history of assault by the parents, then the police would go with me, but they used to stay inside their patrol cars. You just needed sheer power, strong legs and lungs to make it all the way up the forty flights of stairs when your cases were on the top floor of the Red Hook or Marcy Projects. You also needed strong determination to make it through the day in order to keep your job. If you were going to call a certain supervisor or if you were lucky enough to get a court date to go to court the next day after removing children, you'd better be prepared and pray that the call for your court case was before noon. Both the supervisor back at the Child Welfare Office and the judge had a problem with alcohol and were really pathetic after lunch.

I remember being in front of Judge Judy, who now has a successful career as a television judge and not being able to answer her questions as to who had physical custody. I was still wet behind my ears, but I learned every hour, every day, every case was different and the children needed to be protected from those whom were supposed to care for them. I heard the parents' lies regarding broken bones, sexual abuse, and old scars and tried to offer a helping hand. In this big city, I saw poverty, prostitution, disease, and sickness of the mind and body.

Once, I was sent home to de-lice after removing six children that had such a bad lice infestation that there were open sores on their heads. The diaper was stuck to the skin of the baby so bad that chunks of skin came off when I tried to change the diaper, poor baby. He cried for hours, and I tried to comfort him through my sobs. Another time, I was chased down the street by this drunken parent wielding a baseball bat. I was running so fast that I lost my shoes, purse, records, notes, and anything else of value, but I ran to the subway and crawled under the turnstile so fast that I must have looked like an apparition to the other subway riders. My pay was never enough for what I had to do, protect children. Once I testified in court regarding the case of a little four-year-old with cerebral palsy and mild retardation   who   had gonorrhea of the mouth. According to her alcoholic mother, a prostitute, no one in the house could be named as the perpetrator. I spent almost two months picking up that little girl every day in a cab and taking her to different foster homes because New York State was lacking in permanent foster homes for children with such needs. Another time, I removed two beautiful Hispanic girls from their mother. They were so emaciated and skinny that both of them together weighed about forty pounds; one was six and the other was two. I spent the whole day at the office making calls to private agencies and foster homes trying to find permanent placement without being successful, but around 10:00 pm, I found "two beds," the term used by placement and child protective service (CPS) workers when trying to secure a stable placement. Jumping for joy, I called the cab and rode with their measly plastic bag of clothes for almost one hour, only to be told by the foster mother that no one had told her that they were Hispanic girls and that she only took African American little boys. I cried, cajoled, pleaded, and threatened her, but she did not budge. I am sure the little girls were hungry. They were sticking to me like glue, and we were crying after a while, so I picked them up and walked with their belongings to the nearby phone to call a supervisor at home to ask for further instructions. I wanted to take them home so bad, but if I did, I would have lost my job for sure. So I waited by the public phone. There were no cell phones at that time. I waited for another taxi and took the girls to an overnight child protective place in downtown NYC just for the night. The next day before 8:00 am, I was on my way to the city to pick them up and bring them to the office to start the calling cycle all over again. Fortunately, they were able to be placed in a long term loving home where they thrived. Many times, the agency with its lack of workers and resources was accused of furthering the abuse of the children it was supposed to protect, and it was a revolving door for the workers and foster parents alike.

It was the heyday of the crack epidemic, and caseworkers and supervisors alike could be seen rocking the crack babies to sleep and trying to do their best to ease the plight of those little children. At times, taxi drivers would ask me if I was making lots of money because they would not do what I was doing for any money in the world. The protection of children, however, was in my blood. I had been abused in so many ways, sexually, emotionally, physically, and had been so deprived that my mission in life after college was to at least bring protection and smiles to little faces. The glow in those little eyes when you gave them a hug or a kind word meant the world to me. I was a child protective worker for over four years, and I traveled to every county and city in the state, even to a jail in upstate New York. The name of the jail is not important, but I felt I owed to the children in my caseload the opportunity to see their parents even if it meant taking them and their elderly and overwhelmed relatives, mostly grandmothers to spend time with their incarcerated parents. I used to go every other week, giving up my Sundays to pick up the families to a jail upstate so that abused and neglected children could see their loved ones. They deserved to see their parents, albeit if in jail and it was not the little one's fault…it was the most I could do for them in my role as a protective services case manager.

Nowadays, I think that the abuse I experienced as a child was a way to prepare me for my job as an adult. It prepared me to be patient, to look within me and understand the little ones, not to judge the parents or the abusers. It also prepared me to find comforting words, to hug the little ones in silence, and to let them know that someone was there to help them. For me, there was no one to rescue or comfort me, so I became stronger through the abuse so that I could help the weaker ones when they were being abused.

After a while, the job of CPS investigator and dealing with an unruly son was just too overwhelming. While working there, my son became a teen and became disobedient and disrespectful. He would not go to school to hang out with other teens whose mothers were not as involved as me. Since I was working making visits and did not have to be present at the office, after my visits, I would go to my son's school to pick him up just to find out that he had not been in school in days. I spent many afternoons going to parks, friends' homes, local pizza shops, etc., looking for my teenage son. He even got in trouble with the law, and it created havoc with the family. I considered moving out of the "hood" or the second apartment that I rented out from Tina, the owner of the bakery. It was hard because it was a rent-controlled apartment, and I paid so little rent, plus my salary as a case manager was pretty good during those times. I made a lateral transfer to a kinship unit where all the foster parents were relatives of the removed children, and they were all Hispanic families. After about a year of being in the placement kinship unit, I was promoted to supervisor and was responsible for the daily running of the unit and five case managers, the best of the best! I continued working for Social Services until it was time to move to Georgia My husband was then transferred to another army base when the bombshell exploded. Though we both continued working and maintaining our family and our house, we still used recreational drugs until the time Pops took a random drug test given by the army and was almost expelled from the Armed Forces. He spent two years in an army facility in Massachusetts fighting the charges due to an error in the chain of command. These were two long years of separation while he traveled to New York once a month, two long, busy years fighting the system and trying to prove that he had made a mistake and corrected it by attending all kinds of counseling, talking to therapists, working out at whatever he had to work out. I had made a decision that I was going to stop using drugs in order to help him. He had begged me to stop, and we cried in each other's arms. We cried and I told him that I could not quit, but I was stronger than anything ever thrown at me. I stopped using drugs right then and I have never used illicit drugs ever again. He has always thanked me for my decision, but more than anything, I did it for me, for my love for him, for my family, and because I realized I did not need it. I quit cold turkey and said goodbye to that trash forever.

While waiting for his trial, we moved to a three-bedroom house in the East New York section of Brooklyn. I took one last look at the small apartment where I had raised my little ones. With a lump in my throat and tears in my eyes, I said goodbye to the remembrances and good times spent in my second apartment, the railroad apartment, where you could tell time by the rickety, creaking rails of the M train close to Myrtle Avenue. It was where I stayed with my kids and the love of my life for so many years, where I used to look out the third floor window and see the same characters sitting by the doors and holding their wine and beer bottles day after day, and where children played without a care in the world and the women and men would go across the street to Mario's grocery to play their daily numbers.

It was a nice, big comfortable house. Of course, the rent was five times more, but we were very happy. My children each had their own room, we had a larger living room, an enclosed front porch, a separate kitchen, and a spacious bathroom. Also, it was a stone's throw to the elevated J line.

While living at the other apartment we had purchased   a   little

Chihuahua that we named Toby, and he gave us such happy moments and so much love! In this house, Toby would sit by the enclosed porch just to wait for the children arriving from school and for us when we got off the train, going crazy barking and wagging his tail. He was doe-faced, light brown, six pounds, a little dog with pointy ears and the cutest little snout, but boy, did he pack a punch! He was ten pounds of dynamite packed in a little tiny package; he would growl at strangers and bite anyone who dared get close to his girl, Candy. He bit off every toe of every boyfriend she ever had. We lived in this house until we got the news that the trial was finished. The love of my life had won his case and was allowed to stay in the armed forces but was transferred to good ole Georgia in the south. Georgia was on our mind.

Chapter 12

Sweet...Unforgettable Georgia

Goodness gracious! After twenty-five years of living in New York, in the ghettos, living with a chip on your shoulder because you had to be ready to defend yourself at a moment's notice, living with the busiest noises, the sirens, the loud boom boxes, the drugs, the garbage, the rats, the screaming women and children, the gangs, the vendors, the memories of Richie's Candy Store and Shorty getting drunk and being found behind some bush after his mother was seen crying in the corner, seeing the crack heads turn the corner with some stolen prize either in their pocket or their shoulder, the prostitutes, the car fumes, the ethnic cookery smells assaulting your every sense, the hole in the

wall Chinese restaurants, the pizzerias, the delicious fried

plantains, stuffed potatoes, yucca fritters and pork rinds

widely known in New York as cuchifritos, the sounds of

the city, it was time to move on to another life, another

state, another beginning.

Someone had the hardest time with the move,

someone so sweet, so precious, so smart and beautiful—my

daughter said that she was not coming to Georgia, that she

wanted to stay in New York with her aunts or her friends.

Of course, I said no. The love of my life came first in

February 1990, and I was supposed to follow soon after our

daughter finished her ninth grade in middle school. She had

other plans for a while.

The shocking news assaulted me like a hell-bent

tropical hurricane traveling at 150 miles per hour, and I was

right smack in the middle of it. It hit me like a Kansas

tornado. All of the sudden I

felt dizzy, a nauseous feeling took over my entrails, my skin wanted to crawl inside of me, and I stood right in the middle of my daughter's room taking it all in, not knowing what to do, where to turn, how to digest it, where to look and whom to turn to. My precious daughter had ran away and said she was not coming back. Goodness gracious, she was only fourteen and had gone on to the big city, to say goodbye to her friends, to find herself, and again stated she was not moving out of New York. My heart ached upon reading her neatly folded note atop her bed. The world as I had experienced had been turned over, the earth was not on its axis anymore, and my heart had left my body. All this happened in a matter of seconds. I wanted to scream, to cry, and to destroy everything around me. My little girl had left and stated that she was not coming back. My thoughts were racing as I sat in her bed, holding her blanket close to my heart, making believe that she was there, that everything was all right, that she was not gone, her blanket soaking up my tears and somehow telling me that she was OK, that she was only being rebellious for a split second and that any moment now she would walk right in the house as if nothing had happened.

I think those were the worst twenty-four hours of my life, a lost innocent child, lost in the city, a confused young girl who was never left alone unable to sort out her feelings. I imagined the worst had happened to her that the city had swallowed her in one whole piece and was going to spit her out in little chunks. I cried tears as thick as blood that night.

But joy always comes in the morning! Once I showed the note to my son, he immediately made some telephone calls, and, like a ray of sunshine, he went out and in a few hours brought his sister back. All along I have thought that they were in cahoots with each other, that he knew what she was planning all along and held it in reserve so as not to spoil her plans...kids! Siblings will support each other and hide each other's peccadillos! She had spent half of the night and some of the day in her beloved Coney Island with some of her friends. They wanted to be together, to have one last fling before she moved to good ole Georgia, to ride the scary roller coaster one last time, enjoy the old wooden boardwalk and eat one more famous hot dog before leaving what had been her home for the last twelve or so years. She wanted to see her friends one last time, to laugh while the sea breeze from the Atlantic caressed her brown, silky hair, to enjoy all those things that she had enjoyed while growing up in Brooklyn, New York one more time.

Soon, the time to pack up our things and move to Georgia had arrived. During all these months, I had battled and conquered so much, the scars of long fought battles were healing, but so slowly, and it seemed as if my tears would never dry up, as if I had a reservoir full of salty, painful tears ready to burst at a moment's notice, genuine tears that flowed like the Amazon River when the jungle floods and its waters try to destroy everything in its path. Those were the kind of tears that burn your skin, rip your heart in pieces, and bring you to your knees asking all the wrong questions. They are the wrong questions at that time because the right question to ask is what life lesson will I learn out of all this, what is life trying to teach me with its ups and downs, the tears, the heartache, the sleepless nights, the nightmares, the horrible thoughts, what will I learn from all this and how will I use all of it maybe twenty or thirty years from now? How will I utilize this tomorrow and the years ahead? How, my Lord, how?

The time seemed to fly. Weeks, days, hours, and seconds seemed to disappear like a lighting bug that finds itself in a closed fist and suddenly breathes the life-giving breath of air and is gone in a second, like the hazy breath in a cold winter day or a dried up leaf that gently hugs the autumn breeze only to lie in the cold ground hugging the earth, knowing that its life has reached its end. The time to make our move to another state was upon us, and my heart was no longer inside me.

My mind was somewhere over La Guardia Airport, but my part of my heart was in a dark, dingy cell in Riker's Island. My oldest son had been arrested and sentenced to four years in the Queens prison. It ripped my soul having to leave New York and leave my son behind in some obscure jail. Another piece of my heart was going to be ripped apart, another pound of flesh of my flesh, another pint of my blood was going to be spilled. My tears did not flow anymore. The well had dried up, or so I thought until I boarded the plane with my sobbing, heartbroken daughter while our little brown and white Chihuahua, Toby, was caged in the downstairs cabin, barking his head off, wondering where in heavens he was going upon hearing the roar of the plane's engines, and maybe wondering what had happened to his young master.

I felt my heart fly away like the plane, lifting up and reaching toward the blue skies and the cottony clouds while watching the prison in Queens become smaller and smaller, the red brick building resembling doll houses, until my view and my thoughts dissipated like the clouds, to give way to silent sobs and thousands of thoughts of the unknown. There were new horizons coming my way while the drone of the engines kept me awake.

Until I was unable to see the buildings anymore, I was not aware if the height and the clouds were overshadowing my view or if the blurring was caused by my own tears.

Chapter 13

A New Life

The plane arrived in Atlanta, Georgia on time, while the love of my life, as always, dashing and handsome in his camouflaged uniform, waited patiently for us. My sweetheart Pops or Otilio had moved in February and had the house ready for us when we arrived. He helped with the suitcases and hugged our daughter tightly, sensing her unequivocal sadness and despair.

The ocean of people went about their business of collecting baggage, calling taxis, and searching for ground transportation while we gathered our belongings, looking like nomads, out of place. The airport seemed so huge, so packed with travelers, bustling with business, mechanical stairs, and pagers going on and off, foreign languages. Everyone was going someplace while we thought of our new lives in a new state, new house, new friends, and new things to look forward to.

Suddenly, out of the throng of people, out of the thousand noises, we heard the familiar barking of our beloved Toby. We would recognize his bark anywhere. His bark also communicated his confusion of being in a new place, being unfamiliar with the hugeness of it all. His commanding bark called his family to come and get him, to save him from the unknown, to come and let him know that everything was going to be all right. Toby, our furry friend, apparently was also having a hard time with the move. Upon arriving near his crate, he could tell that his sojourn into the unknown was over, and he wagged his tail, his barking resounding all over the airport and Clayton County.

We had arrived at our new abode...a brand new, clean, tidy house in the outskirts of Clayton County...resembling a doll's house ready to welcome its new denizens.

It was summer 1990, and I was still wiping tears from so many memories, so much heartache. My coworkers at Social Services gave me a beautiful going away party. I had received so many flowers and gifts that I had to call a taxi that day to bring me home. The gifts and celebration came from true friends who appreciated all my hard work. Even the foster parents gathered together to make my last day an unforgettable one. It was a bittersweet move for me. In one way, I was so happy I was joining the love of my life at our new house; in another, I was melancholic at leaving what had been my home for the last twenty-five years, leaving my family, my friends, my job, and, most of all, leaving a piece of me locked up in the infamous prison overlooking the grand lagoon at Flushing Bay. I know that my daughter felt the same way, and I was at a loss for words. I just held her close and whispered in her ear that everything was going to be all right.

But we were in Georgia, ready to start our new lives in our new house, ready to tackle whatever the future held in store for us, and ready to tell the world that whatever challenges came our way, we would not allow them to take us down. We were ready to overcome any tribulations and trials lurking around the corner.

Summer of 1990 was upon us, and we certainly did not enjoy our summer. We sent for our seven-year-old nephew and our five-year-old niece so that our daughter would have company during the summer. My daughter was miserable and spent all day locked in her room. The two kids kept knocking at her door, and her screams telling them to leave her alone could be heard all over the subdivision. The little ones tried to entertain themselves by playing outside and making friends with the other neighborhood children. We attended some fairs and festivals in Piedmont Park and took the children to the nearby pool in Ft. Gillem. Fourth of July was a blast at

Lenox Mall, and the fireworks were awesome. The kids enjoyed each and every one of them.

Our belongings literally took the whole summer to arrive. We looked like little anthills during the night. The little ones had comforters and sleeping bags set up on the floor of the guest room, and we slept on the floor. It was a blessing not to get up to make up beds in the mornings.

We conspired to help our daughter by enrolling her in the local modeling school; apparently, it helped her come out of her shell. We would take her every Saturday to downtown Atlanta for her classes, and she enjoyed every minute of it. There were girls coming all the way from Tennessee and Alabama every Saturday to learn proper modeling techniques. They would do their own hair and makeup and "would strut their stuff," or so they said. We spent a small fortune on classes, photo shoots, gas, lunches, etc., but today, I think that it was worth every dollar spent. Our beloved daughter soon made friends, and being locked in her room soon became a thing of the past. She was more confident and outgoing and even made some friends in the neighborhood. The summer was coming to an end, and she was looking forward to attending her new high school, meeting new friends, and tackling her classes. She had always been a straight A student, and I was confident that the new school would not pose a challenge for her. I was right. Our niece and nephew would soon be on their merry way to their respective homes—one was flying to Puerto Rico and the other one to New York, and I dreaded the possibility of staying home alone in a big house.

I was looking forward to finding a job, but faced a huge problem: no car. In Georgia, you need a reliable automobile even to go to the corner store, which was a couple of miles away. In my line of work, I needed a car and a Georgia driver's license badly. In other words, I needed a car in order to get a job. Pops bought me a hoopdie or old clunker of a car as they say and parked it in the driveway, saying, "Here is your car. You want a job? Then drive your car!" I had a license from New York but the thought of being behind a wheel scared the wits out of me. I used the New York's driver license for identification purposes. After trying to return a rental car in Brooklyn, New York, and putting so many dents due to my lack of driving skills and practicing turning into neighborhood streets and paying thousands of dollars for the car rental, I vowed never to get behind the steering wheel of a car ever again. The traffic and the streets of New York always put a holy fear in me and was terrified of driving in New York, I still abhor driving in New York…don't know why! …but I needed to work!

All things happen for a purpose, and it just so happened that we never owned a washer and dryer. We were still in a New York mode of thinking and did not see a need to get a washing

200

machine...and the dirty clothes kept piling up! I would go outside and look at the old driving machine just sitting in the driveway, go around it, touch it, smell the fumes, kick the tires...just tried to be friends with it, but soon found out that it was not moving by itself. It would not take me anywhere. It was a massive old Oldsmobile that terrorized the bejesus out of me, but it was going to be my lifesaver if I ever gathered enough courage to get inside, start the huge machine and get to know it. Another challenge facing me was that those fears deep within me kept raising their ugly heads, they became giants trying to keep me from becoming successful, but I had regained confidence, I was starting a new life and vowed to not let them me down...I had my slingshot ready!

I said to myself that there were too many clothes to wash by hand and it was not fair for the love of my life to come home after a hard day at work to take me wash clothes at the Laundromat, so I would go outside, load the bags of dirty clothes and sit inside the hot car, thinking, thinking what to do next, start the car? Drive it around the corner and come back, go to the small plaza five miles away, or just go back inside and wash clothes in the sink? The last option did not seem like my cup of tea anymore, so I just started the car. The roar of its engine drowned my thoughts and sent me in a sweating and shaking frenzy, my legs unable to reach for the brakes and my hands unable to open the door. I felt trapped inside the machine and only wanted to get out, run out, and hide in the safety of my home. And I did. I left the car running, wasting gas while I ran inside, car door ajar, the door to the house ajar, while I sat in the sofa looking around like a mad woman, running alternatively to the window and to the door looking at the car, silly me...as if the car was going anywhere! Fear and panic had settled in and I was miserable...tears flowed down my face and I needed to do what I knew had to be done...I had to defeat the giants within. Afterwards, I would go outside to turn the engine off and load the dirty clothes back in the house. A whole week went by with the same scenario, but my love needed his clean underwear! What is a woman to do?

Until one day I faced the monster head on…by not loading the clothes and detergents and going around the corner over and over again. I knew then that I had conquered a hurdle and spent two days doing nothing but going around in circles in the cul-de-sac trying to get my bearings and finding my comfort zone. The next week I was brave enough that I dared go the nearby Laundromat by myself, the demon of driving a car had been put to rest! I had been victorious once again, and nothing was going to stop me from looking for a job!

I started by filling out an application and sending my resume to the Georgia State Personnel Department. After six weeks of nervously waiting for a response, I obtained a score and a notice that my application had been sent to various nearby counties for consideration of employment. I was still terrified because the jobs that I had applied for were case manager jobs, and the main requirement of these jobs was to make home visits to ensure the safety and well-being of the children in the caseload or to make home visits to prospective foster/adoptive parents. What a requirement for a new driver like me! Toughest decision that I had to make, but I started to receive notices of application approval. The telephone would not stop ringing, and I was delighted to agree to job interviews. The first county to call me was Fulton, and I interviewed with the Placement and with the Adoption/Recruitment Units. I was hired by the Adoption Unit. Terror took over my emotions when I realized that I had been hired and that I would be making home visits in the largest county in the state of Georgia. I had to conduct not only home visits, but I had to teach foster and adoption classes and place children for adoption. This was a big change from when I was in Brooklyn, New York, going into crack houses, or projects that were forty stories high in the Red Hook and Bushwick sections of New York and traveling by bus, taxi, and train to get to see the children in my caseload and the foster parents. I also had to go to Family Court and meet with strung out parents who swore that it was never their fault their children were neglected and abused. This was a long trek and a big change indeed, but I had a job in Georgia! The adoption unit was considered the crème of the crop, the cushiest position because you had no contact with the birth parents, the court appearances and testimonies were minimal, and one of the greatest rewards was to see families being formed.

I worked in the Adoption Unit until 2001, and then I had to take a leave of absence due to needed surgery. After I went back, I realized that the drive through almost four counties to get to work in Fulton County was just too much, so I applied for a victim advocate job in Clayton County, and I was hired. This job entailed working with the victims of crimes committed by juveniles and ensuring that restitution was being paid by the perpetrators. It was very difficult to get any restitution to the victims because most of the perpetrators were teenagers without a source of income. I don't ever remember getting any restitution paid to the victims. Most of the time, my office was packed with victims trying to get some money for their pain and suffering, so I often advised them to sue in a higher court or to try to reach an agreement with the parents. It was a catch 22 situation, however, because since the children committing the crimes were underage, I could not divulge their names or any other identifying information to the victims. The most I could do was lend a listening ear to the victims and testify on their behalf as to how their lives were impacted and changed by the crimes committed against them. It was a very lonely and hard job indeed. I lasted a year in that position and soon afterwards, went back to a foster care position in the county where I lived.

It was also 2001 when we moved from Clayton County to Spalding County to a house that we built with lots of love, tears, sacrifices, heartaches, and lots of laughter. Our dream house was built on five acres of beautiful rolling hills and fertile farmland. Our lot was one of the most strikingly beautiful due to the tree line in the front. In the back, we had access to a huge county lake well stocked with bass and bream. It even had some wild Bradford pear trees in the back along with muscadine grapes, persimmons, and numerous raspberries and blueberries vines. Along the half mile entrance, we discovered beautiful passion fruit flowers that gave wonderful wild passion fruits, and we even had some wild crepe myrtles and pink and white dogwoods. Our land was a heavenly place. From the very first minute we laid our eyes on it, from the bend about two miles away, one chilly October afternoon, when the colors of autumn were doing their last dance of the year, when the trees were changing to their best fall colors, when the birds went down south and you only saw a lone duck or heron fly by, when the leaves danced among themselves, trying to outdo each other in their passionate dance, we knew it was our promised land. It was our dream land, our treasured paradise nestled among a crystal clear lake, with fruit trees, wild flowers, and strong oak trees, where the deer, foxes, wild turkeys, doves, ducks, rabbits, and colorful snakes also decided to live and raise their young. It was where creepy crawlers enjoyed the cool mornings and tried to avoid the hot summer afternoons. It was our dream home where dreams came alive, and where we planted beautiful gardens, where we nurtured all kinds of birds and animals, and where we carefully laid the stones for our desert garden featuring all kind of succulent plants. We fell in love with that land and carefully watched every aspect of the construction, from the sections that were cordoned off specifying the building site, to the construction of our beautiful and huge porch, our Japanese style pergola, the concrete paved walkway, and the laying of the slate gray stones to beautify our porch.

The tears flowed when we encountered stumbling blocks while trying to get building permits, grading the land, and getting permits for the well, the septic tank, and the light pole. There were so many permits that were required. Also we had to secure the construction loan. And we had to select every detail inside and outside the house, from the roof shingles to the color of the shutters to the inside color of the walls, the cabinets, light fixtures, etc. It was really a labor of love, but I promised that I was not going to ever build a house from scratch ever again. But we did in 2001, and it was finally turnkey ready by the beginning of autumn of that year. We slept on the floor of our new house built with love and sweat the first day we received the keys after the closing. We were so tired that we parked the moving truck outside and just dropped on the floor out of sheer exhaustion.

That was the house that the Lord provided for us, and we were so grateful. We wanted to dedicate our home to the Lord and invited the whole congregation, which at that time numbered about 50-60 people and some friends and relatives. We wanted to show our friends and family what we had been blessed with along with the labor we had expended with almost a year of supervising, taking pictures, and coming to the house almost every day. It was a beautiful, well-built house, and that Saturday morning we got up early to prepare breakfast, get fresh flowers and decoration, set up the tables and the candles, to make sure the house was ready to be shared. We wanted to share how the joy of owning a house built from scratch could be mutually shared with those we loved, to share the Lord's blessings, and give the house back to the Lord. The minutes passed, and they became hours. We kept looking at the road trying to make out a familiar car, looking at the dust left by the pickup trucks and cars as they hurried down along the dirt road, looking long and scanning the sky for a familiar sound, but the sounds were not heard. The cars were not seen coming down the dirt road, the food got cold, and the delicious smells of fresh omelets, bacon, and fresh fruits no longer filled the air. And the tears flowed, heavy tears of disillusionment, tears that burned our skin while trickling down, but we had a house dedication that morning. There were two souls holding hands and going over every room, every piece of furniture, every decoration, every picture, and everything in the house was separated for the glory of our Lord. We had a house dedication and housewarming party that morning, just the two of us, and it felt good. Tears of disappointment were transformed into tears of joy as we held a housewarming party all by ourselves, and we were able to feel all the warmth and love as it emanated from our lovely house.

Chapter 14

Farewell …My Queen…A Seed is Planted

The five women stood there for what it seemed like an eternity, forever, each one of them lost in her own thoughts and pondering what had just happened. They were huddled together, yet their souls looked lost like a bird flipping about, separated from their flock. They each looked around amidst the sparse living room which seemed to sink in under their feet with each passing microsecond.

Their glassy, tear-filled eyes took in every moment, trying to grasp every memory, memento, the special moments each had with the loving soul that had just departed toward her heavenly mansion. Each of them was struggling with the pain, their thoughts, and the realization that their mother had just gone on to Heaven, to that beautiful place well above the sky, that wonderful faraway place that not even the strongest birds can reach, a special place only available to the soul, where everyone aims to go one day. It is the place where peace and tranquility coexist in an unknown way. They were dumbfounded and terrified at the loneliness around them and at a loss for words. Not a sound was uttered for what it seemed like an eternity, but in reality only a split second had passed. All of a sudden, like the foggy, hazy light of a faraway lighthouse and the thundering, forceful whistle of an old winding My forgotten freight train, a sound that silently starts to fade away, they heard the sounds of one of their sister's voice, telling them not to cry, that the moment had arrived and that their mother had departed to a better place. They were still in shock, their arms languidly hanging like dead branches, like that lonely autumn leaf still hanging on to the dead branch. Their bodies quivered and trembled, and it seemed as if their words were being held hostage at their throats by an unknown force. There were five of them, five different worlds. The person responsible for their uniqueness, their differences, and the glue holding them together had just come apart, and they felt so alone.

The funeral and the ceremony at her final resting place was a beautiful event. There was a long line of automobiles, and the police escort did not make it any easier. She was finally laid to rest in a queenly fashion. She lived like a peasant, but was buried like a queen. She had not only one, but three pastors at her wake and burial. The flowers, the poems, the farewell letters all brought it home. The five sisters lacked energy and were somber, but the grief and pain was still there. The Queen had gone home to meet her King. Farewell, farewell to our lovely, beautiful, strong, sad queen.

Chapter 15

Dreams Along the Way...

May 24th, 2012

8:15 am

Today I woke up around 7:30, and as always, I took the little, four-legged, furry friend out so he could do his business and rushed back inside. It had rained all night, and the wet soil was sticking to my house shoes like gum sticks on dentures. The puppy's belly was wet and sticky. After he did his thing, I picked him up, came inside, and wiped his furry legs clean. I felt so tired and listless that I crawled back to bed, but I told myself that just another ten or fifteen minutes of snooze wouldn't hurt. So I went back to bed, and it did not felt like a dream but more like an ecstatic out of body experience. I was happy, happier than I have ever been. I closed my eyes and saw the most wonderful, out-of-this-world events, and heard the most familiar, sweetest voices. The visions that were shown to me were so indescribable that I will do my best to describe them in words. It is impossible to describe a beautiful, gorgeous painting, but that is what I will try to do.

I was in a carnival with lots of people just walking around and having fun. Tiny and gigantic balloons with rainbows of yellow, red, turquoise, lavender, purple, all shades of orange and blues, and green colors were everywhere. A galore of tent kiosks of all shapes and colors were lining the streets. Vendors were selling all types of wares, screaming at the top of their lungs trying to get the passersby to come into their tent and try their luck at the games or to buy their products. They were screaming so hard you could actually see their veins like rolled coils popping out of their necks and their faces contorted in a phantasmagorical grimace. But we were not paying attention to any of the activity around us. We were together, and that seemed to

217

be the most important thing. We were in the carnival but in our own little world. I was with my hubby, holding hands and just walking along. We were laughing so hard that tears were rolling down our faces, but those were tears of joy and contentment, of happiness, of remembrances, bittersweet tears, and tears of a lifetime together, and he was glowing with happiness. We looked so happy together, holding each other, kissing each other. We had no cares or worries, and it seemed as if the world was ours to conquer. In those moments I felt such tenderness, such love for my husband, and it was like our souls had been fashioned into one. We were in one spirit, and we were walking together.

We saw this little green booth that was advertising the winning of a watch as a grand prize, and since I know that my husband loves watches, we looked at each other and instantly knew that he would play this game just to win the watch. Or was it to win us some more time together? I don't know, but in the roulette of life, time is precious and you just cannot assign a price to time spent with loved ones. Anyway, the object of the game was to swirl this twine attached to the most beautiful opal Technicolor large round shell, and at the end of the twine was another little shell, exactly the same as the large shell, but tiny in size. In a split second, with one twist of his hand, my husband got the little shell inside the large one, and we both laughed so hard our laughter surrounded the whole carnival. The young lady, dressed in green and resembling Tinker Bell with long, blond, flowing curls, gave us a smile and handed a spectacular emerald green wristwatch that seemed larger than life itself, encrusted with large green emeralds, to my husband. Emerald green, the color of hope, was with us, as we happily ran away from the booth giggling all the way and carrying on. It was the largest emerald green watch I have ever seen in my husband's hand, and as I looked back, the booth was vanishing in thin air.

And then we both saw the thing—a very large snake, with brown, tan, red, and black stripes just slithering along the dirty floor. For a fleeting instant, its greenish, beady, devilish eyes were locked with mine and I felt fear, indescribable fear, trembling and paralyzing fear. It seemed to move so fast for being such a large reptile. As it slinked and hissed along its way toward us, people panicked and ran, opening up a space along the way, but its eyes were locked with mine. It was coming directly toward me with a purpose. I felt its destroying force. It appeared to me that the snake was about one hundred feet long, and it probably weighed about a thousand pounds. Its neck was the size of a rain barrel at its widest point, and its tail whipped back and forth. Every time it whipped its tail, tongues of fire came out, engulfing everything in its path. It was a monstrous, menacing, and destructive force, and it was coming like a speeding moving truck toward me. So we ran for our lives, until we stopped and the monster snake was no longer there. There was a freak sideshow going on, however, on a platform, and thousands of people were surrounding the platform waiting for the show to start. In our attempt to escape the fury of our persecutor, we mingled with the crowd. The star of the show was a beautiful woman. Her calf-length hair was bright and long, the most beautiful blondish gold, and her hair was flowing in the air, undulating with every stroke of wind. Her skin was like burnished bronze, and her eyes were big and blue, but she had this treacherous look in her eyes and immediately seemed to pick me out of a crowd of thousands. She kept looking at me; it was like I had been captured by just her eyes, and I could not get away. I felt an unusual power to gaze away and not get sucked in by her powerful stare, but I just could not keep my eyes off her. When I looked back, she was reclining in a sofa, her back to me. She had turned back into a snake, but she had the body of the woman and the face of the snake. She had a tattoo of the spinal cord along her back. As she moved and contorted in a frenzy, her tattoo seemed to burst into life, moving up and down her spine, hypnotizing the onlookers. People started falling at the foot of the platform in a zombie-like trance, trembling, shaking, and having seizures, screaming all kinds of obscenities. As I watched this infernal show, my heart pumping so fast it was almost popping out of my chest cavity, I told myself, "Run like crazy, run like you never ran before, run and don't look back, run for your life. Run! Run! Run!" So, I ran, and my husband was right behind me until we both came to a tall fence with entwined vines and ivy all over. I gathered all my strength, and with an invisible force carrying me, holding hands with my husband, perspiration bathing both of us, we took a flying leap and made it safely to the other side, the carnival freak show and the infernal serpent behind us.

As I went over the fence, I found myself in a local clinic, exhausted and lying in a waiting room. People in white clinical gowns were coming and going around conducting their business, not paying attention to me. I was trying laboriously to breathe and regain my strength. I was lying in a white hospital bed, but I was also looking out a little window in the room, looking as my body lay in the little bed. Everything in the room was white with a strange glow, like a hazy, white, ghoulish fog, but I had been forgotten. I kept screaming at people to attend to me, but my screams fell unto deaf ears. I felt so alone then until someone came to get my pulse, looked at me, and ran out. I could not understand her words, but lots of doctors came to look at me but left and did not say anything. It was a strange feeling. I was looking inside a window, and I was also seeing myself in a hospital bed. I was out of my own body! Very strange indeed! From the little glass-paned window, I saw a fire truck turn the corner and heard sirens, but could not talk. I somehow knew, however, that they were coming to attend to me. I saw a woman in a white robe come to me, touch my hand and then put a warm blanket over me. I then relaxed and let go. It seemed like I was floating in space, weightless. As I floated off, this feeling of unexplained peace, tranquility, and restful lightness took over, and I felt I was levitating off the bed. I could hear the news on the television in the room, and the picture was the sharpest, clearest picture I have ever seen. All of a sudden, the picture turned fuzzy and snowy with lots of static, which sounded like a radio station out of tune, bringing back memories of an old black and white television from the fifties, those that had only one or two channels that went off at midnight. There was a sound and a click and all of a sudden, I saw the pictures of my loved ones that have passed away. I saw my father-in-law Otilio, smiling, laughing, and carrying on about his fishing expeditions and the length of his latest catch. I saw my exmother-in-law, Maria Alejandro, so young, so peppy, cracking jokes and laughing. I also saw her son, my son's father, Angel the Red One, as healthy as ever, with his dry sense of humor telling unending stories of his conquests. Best of all, I saw my beautiful mother, Marina, her long, black, waist-length hair with its matching white streak, her beautiful dress; she was happy and so beautiful. She looked like a Hollywood model, and they were talking, laughing, and carrying on. They were not in the television picture at the same time, however. It was like an old black and white Johnny Carson show. They were his guests, and each of them were being interviewed individually, each talking into the camera one at a time, telling how good they felt and how happy they are now.

I heard my son's angelic voice, telling the nurse or doctor or a person in the room about how sick I had been and what my symptoms were. Then I also saw the door open and the EMS personnel came in, carrying their bags and coming to see me. This gentle Caucasian guy dressed in orange overalls with black large EMS letters on the back came over, held my nose, and opened my mouth, I think to give me mouth-to mouth-resuscitation. Every time he breathed into my mouth, I felt like the rush of an ocean inside me, thousands of gallons of water rushing in and rushing out, rushing in and rushing out but finally, the water rushed out and did not came back in. The guy checked my pulse again and told me to get up and go with him on a special trip. He was so loving, so kind and understanding, gentleness emanated from his every action, and love was evident in every one of his acts toward me.

There was this long walkway, and it seemed to be in the last resort that we stayed, but the stairs in the resort were hanging from the sky, never touching the sand nor the floor. I kept following the kind, white man in the orange overalls, not looking back.

While walking I saw my daughter, Candy, the picture of health with the biggest beach bag full of beach toys and souvenirs, and she was talking with her best friend, Melanie, about her vacation. She was glowing with exuberant happiness. She looked and sounded happy. She was telling Melanie that she was OK. I also saw my sisters carrying on about their daily business, and they were laughing. It seemed like in my dream everyone was happy and laughing, and I met my husband again, happy as a lark without a care in the world. I told him that he could not come on the trip that the white man in the orange overalls was taking me on, that it was my trip but the he could accompany me halfway. We went into this boat, and all of a sudden the ocean came into view.

It was the bluest and largest ocean I have ever seen. The water at times looked bluish and green, different shades of blue, green, and turquoise, and it seemed like the waves were gold and sometimes silvery, the calmest ocean ever, the most beautiful ocean that anyone can imagine! As I put my hand in the ocean, the water felt soft and warm. I could see the shimmering glitter of different hues of silver and gold, multicolored specks of light bouncing off my hands and fingers, and the feelings of peace, happiness, and calm solitude overcame my senses. I floated off, being lifted off higher and higher, like a helium balloon flying off into space that you look up at it until it blends with the sky, appearing as a little dot up above and then you don't see it anymore. That's how I felt, lovingly carried by the ocean waves and the air, floating off to an unknown place. I was by myself, glancing occasionally at the little boat disappearing in the distance until I could no longer see the boat nor the loving person inside it, and I was certain that person was no longer shedding tears. He was happy for me.

Upon awakening and looking at the clock, it was 8:15 am.

Was this a dream or a futuristic vision of things to come? I don't have the foggiest idea, but certain things in my life have been made clearer and more certain.

Now I don't have a doubt that I have lived a purposeful, meaningful life. I have loved and been loved and have experienced life with a fullness and joy that few people have experienced. I have conquered wickedness and evil and have the taste of victory in my life and my spirit. I know that my dear loved ones that have departed this earthly world are united and glorified in heaven. My loved ones, the ones that I have shared my love, my tears, my life, my ups and downs, my victories and challenges with will be OK long after I am gone. I am certain that I will continue to live forever in their hearts. Most of all, however, I know what waits for me after I have crossed that vast, shimmering golden ocean. The Lord told me once at my mother's deathbed, "Don't worry, my daughter, I am with you." and I believed

Him when He said this. His words were for my mom's ears as she awaited her glorious moment, my sisters as they dealt with their pain and suffering, and for me during my most difficult time. I have taken His words and his promises into my heart, and I know that all will be well within my soul.

Chapter 16

Rejoicing Comes in the Morning

A simple story with a purpose, a labor of love, has been accomplished. It is time to rejoice and time to reminisce about those events in my life that shaped me, molded me, taught me, and helped me become a stronger person. My race has just begun, and the road ahead looms larger than life itself. I don't see these past events as drawbacks or heavy boulders or monoliths in my life. Instead, I now see them as golden opportunities, chances that my Supreme and Glorious Creator has gifted me with to assist me in my quest, and along the way, I have become a better person, a stronger human being, a woman of substance and courage. I have seen evil at its ugliest, and I have conquered it. As a result, I have been able to obtain the peace and the joy that surpasses all understanding.

CPSIA information can be obtained at www.ICGtesting.com
Printed in the USA
LVOW05s0224071214

417588LV00017B/1568/P